WOODWORKER'S
# GARDEN
# PROJECTS

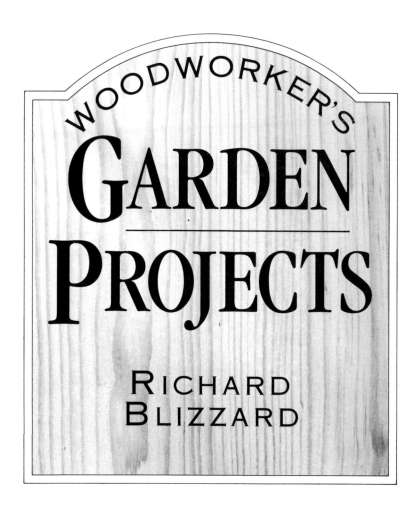

# WOODWORKER'S
# GARDEN
# PROJECTS

R ICHARD
B LIZZARD

HarperCollins*Publishers*

First published in 1993 by
HarperCollins Publishers
London

A CIP catalogue record for this book is available
from the British Library.

ISBN 0 00 412654 8

Designed by Peter Butler
Photography by Ron Sutherland
Diagrams by Dave Scammell
Artwork research by Mervyn Hurford

Typeset in Gill Sans by Phoenix Photosetting, Chatham, Kent
Colour reproduction in Hong Kong
Printed and bound in Great Britain by Butler & Tanner Ltd,
Frome and London

# CONTENTS

*For the more skilled woodworker

# FOREWORD

I have enjoyed making the projects in this book and I do hope that the variety of things made will encourage and help you to get started.

If you are a keen gardener and feel just a little bit daunted by some of the projects – don't be. Start with something simple and useful, and with a first project successfully completed the confidence will grow to enable you to tackle others.

I am hoping that for many of you who watch birds and other small mammals in your garden, you will take up the challenge to build all kinds of animal shelters, not just for the owl and other birds.

The projects have been carefully chosen and any one of them will enhance the beauty of your home and garden.

I wish you many happy hours of woodworking.

*Richard Blizzard*
*1993*

# ACKNOWLEDGEMENTS

I am very grateful to the following companies and individuals who have given me their full support and cooperation throughout the preparation of this book.

**The Swedish Finnish Timber Council,** 17 Exchange, Retford, Nottinghamshire, England, DN22 6BZ: Peter Grimsdale and Jack Baird, for supplying Nordic red- and whitewood.

**Makita Electric (UK) Ltd,** 8 Finway, Dallow Road, Luton, Bedfordshire, England, LUI 1TR: Gary Morikawa, Derrick Marshall, Bruce Smith, Carole Chant and Terry Bicker, who made available the machines from the Makita Pro range of tools.

**Nettlefolds Ltd,** Woden Road, Wednesbury, West Midlands, England, WS10 7TT: Janet Webber, who supplied all the zinc-plated screws, coach-bolts and coach-screws.

**Humbrol Ltd,** Marfleet, Kingston-upon-Hull, North Humberside, England, HU9 5NE: Tony Allen, who supplied all the waterproof glues and non-toxic childproof paints.

**Metpost,** Mardy Road, Cardiff, Wales, CF3 8EQ: David Maas, Jason Cole and Tim Evans, who supplied the spiked steel sockets with driving tool used in the Garden Fence, Play Tower and Barbecue Shelter projects in this book. I thank them too for the border roll lawn edging that was used to set off the borders around the Barbecue Shelter.

**Cuprinol Ltd,** Adderwell, Frome, Somerset, England, BA11 1NL: Peter Hunt and Graham Howard, for the supply of wood preservatives and exterior varnishes, and for their assistance with photography.

**Evode Ltd,** Common Road, Stafford, England, ST16 3EH: Fiona Ellis, for the supply of varnishes and wood stains.

**Record Marples,** Parkway Works, Sheffield, England: Peter Peck, for first-class hand tools.

**The Royal Society for the Protection of Birds,** The Lodge, Sandy, Bedfordshire, England, SG19 2DL: Mrs D. Ryal, for help and assistance with information on nestboxes. Details of a number of bird boxes not featured in this book are available from the Society, including boxes for birds found outside Britain and Europe. Also write to the above address for details of how to become a member of the RSPB.

**The British Trust for Ornithology,** The Nunnery, Nunnery Place, Thetford, Norfolk, England, IP24 2PU: for information on nestboxes. The Trust will provide detailed leaflets on a range of bird boxes, e.g. for Kestrels, Tawny and Barn Owls etc.

**Polly Powell,** Senior Commissioning Editor, HarperCollins/ Collins Leisure, for lots of good ideas – and for being a good listener when things went wrong!

**Barbara Dixon,** for finalising text and drawings, and coordinating the final stages.

**Robin Wood and Angela Witherby,** for keeping an eye on us all!

**Mervyn Hurford and Dave Scammell,** for drawings, cutting lists, . . . and burning the midnight oil.

**Ron Sutherland,** for taking the photographs.

**Peter Butler,** for art directing the book.

**Margaret Ward,** for unscrambling my handwritten text.

**T. Butt & Son,** Stroud, Gloucestershire, England: builders merchants, together with their yard foreman and his team of lorry drivers, for faithfully delivering vast quantities of wood so quickly and efficiently.

# FURNITURE AND GARDEN ORNAMENTS

TO SIT IN THE GARDEN ENJOYING A DRINK, WHILE LUNCH IS
COOKING NICELY ON THE BARBECUE, IS A REAL PLEASURE –
AND EVEN MORE SATISFYING WHEN YOU HAVE MADE THE
CHAIRS AND TABLE FROM WHICH YOU'LL BE EATING. ALSO
INCLUDED IN THIS SECTION IS A BARBECUE SHELTER, TO
ENSURE YOU ENJOY AN UNINTERRUPTED MEAL.

# BARBECUE
# SHELTER

IT IS A BEAUTIFUL SUMMER EVENING. THE BEEFBURGERS ARE
BROWNING NICELY, THE BACON IS COOKED, AND THE FAMILY IS
ALL READY TO ENJOY AN OUTDOOR MEAL. THEN A COLD
WIND BLOWS UP, CLOUDS ZOOM ACROSS THE SKY, AND THE
FIRST FEW SPOTS OF RAIN START TO FALL. IF YOU HAVE EVER
EXPERIENCED THIS SORT OF SITUATION, YOU WILL APPRECIATE
JUST HOW WONDERFUL IT CAN BE TO BE ABLE TO FINISH THE
COOKING AND ENJOY THE MEAL, IN THE DRY AND OUT OF THE
WIND, WHILE THE ELEMENTS DO THEIR WORST OUTSIDE.

**P**lease don't think that the measurements and dimensions I give for this project must be applied rigidly. No – the shelter I describe here is meant as a basis for construction: you can add to it or alter its dimensions to suit your own garden. You might, for example, consider fixing a sheet of corrugated perspex to the roof decking, which would really keep you dry through any summer storm. You might consider wooden benches, or even fixed seating. With or without such additions, this shelter is not difficult to build – and, as usual in this book, I have avoided the use of the traditional methods of jointing.

But before you start your woodworking there are several points that do require thinking about. The assembled construction is big and heavy: you will have to find a suitable location for putting it together, and from which it can reasonably easily be transported to its final site.

To build it, you need a large, flat surface – the drive, or the lawn, perhaps. If you decide for convenience to build it in the garage, make sure that you will be able to get it out of the garage doors even in the form of the initial framework

(and remember that some suburban car insurance policies are valid only if the car stays in a garage at night). Check that if you build it at the front of the house there will be room – without the need for razing walls or uprooting trees – to transport it round to the back, if that is where it's to go.

There is an equally important need for discretion right from the beginning in the choice of the wood to be used.

## STARTING OUT

**1** At the woodyard, select eight main upright posts. Reject any that have the slightest suggestion of a twist.

**2** Back in your workyard (garage, drive, lawn, helicopter-pad . . .), clamp the posts together in order to mark across all eight at once in pencil where at the top the top planks are to go, and where at the bottom the spiked steel sockets that will hold the posts in the ground are to come up to.

**Find a quiet corner in the garden to set up your Barbecue Shelter. Paving slabs make an ideal base.**

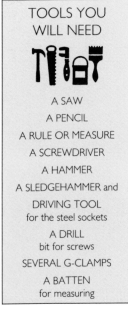

## TOOLS YOU
## WILL NEED

A SAW
A PENCIL
A RULE OR MEASURE
A SCREWDRIVER
A HAMMER
A SLEDGEHAMMER and
DRIVING TOOL
for the steel sockets
A DRILL
bit for screws
SEVERAL G-CLAMPS
A BATTEN
for measuring

## MATERIALS

Wood:

  eight posts

  six planks (to connect

    posts horizontally)

  planks (to act as roofing)

  battens

  ship lapboarding

Zinc-plated Supascrews

Nails

Post-fixing steel sockets

  with spiked tip

Wood preservative

## SAFETY TIP

Battery powered
screwdriver/drills are the
safest outdoor electric tools
to use – no cables to tangle
up and no chance of
electrocution.

ASSEMBLING THE PARTS

**3** The next step is to make three individual pieces of framework. Two of the frames are to have three upright posts, one at each end and one at the centre; and the third frame – which is to be the middle one – has only a post at both ends. Each frame's uprights are connected by planks screwed horizontally across at the top, one on each side.

Make one framework at a time. With the posts lying flat, position a plank each side at the top. Attach a light batten also horizontally across the bottom (but above the mark for the spiked sockets), using a few G-clamps. The batten helps to keep the construction temporarily rigid, but will be removed at a late stage. Make sure the posts and the planks of the framework are properly square to each other (by checking with another batten that the measurement diagonally between bottom corner and top corner is consistent between posts), and – after any vital adjustments – mark in pencil where posts and planks should meet.

Now drill pilot holes for the screws through the upper plank at the top into the posts. Because the screws are necessarily large for this project, pilot holes are essential or the torque required to drive in the screws might well prove too strenuous.

**4** Drive the screws through the plank into the posts. For strength, the screws ought to be of a fairly hefty size – length 9 cm (3½ in), diameter 4 mm ($\frac{1}{6}$ in, No. 10) or 6 mm (¼ in, No. 8) – and should have the cross-head, not the older single slot in the head, for security and ease while screwing in with strength.

Screw the light batten in position at the bottom too.

Now – with an assistant – turn the frame over. Then attach the other plank at the top in the same way (drilling the pilot holes first, screws afterward), making sure that the pencil marks are observed and that posts and plank remain square. You should then have one frame of the three.

## BARBECUE SHELTER CUTTING LIST

### CENTRAL FRAME

**Verticals** 2 off 2362 × 73 × 73 mm (93 × 2⅞ × 2⅞ in) timber

**Top cross members** 2 off 3353 × 124 × 22 mm (132 × 4⅞ × ⅞ in) timber

**Central packer** 1 off 330 × 73 × 73 mm (13 × 2⅞ × 2⅞ in) timber

**Assembly tie member** 1 off 2883 × 149 × 22 mm (113½ × 5⅞ × ⅞ in) timber

### PANELLED END FRAME

**Verticals** 3 off 2362 × 73 × 73 mm (93 × 2⅞ × 2⅞ in) timber
2 off 1080 × 73 × 73 mm (42½ × 2⅞ × 2⅞ in) timber

**Top cross members** 2 off 3353 × 124 × 22 mm (132 × 4⅞ × ⅞ in) timber

**Rear tie member** 1 off 2883 × 64 × 22 mm (113½ × 2½ × ⅞ in) timber

**Sills** 2 off 1332 × 86 × 22 mm (52⁷⁄₁₆ × 3⅜ × ⅞ in) timber

**Cladding** 10 off 2883 × 121 × 12 mm (113½ × 4¾ × ½ in) ship lapboarding

### LADDER END FRAME

**Verticals** 3 off 2362 × 73 × 73 mm (93 × 2⅞ × 2⅞ in) timber
4 off 2203 × 47 × 47 mm (86¾ × 1⅞ × 1⅞ in) timber

**Top cross members** 2 off 3353 × 124 × 22 mm (132 × 4⅞ × ⅞ in) timber

**Lower tie member** 1 off 2883 × 64 × 22 mm (113½ × 2½ × ⅞ in) timber

**Horizontal slats** 5 off 902 × 117 × 22 mm (35½ × 4⅝ × ⅞ in) timber

### SIDE INFILL

**Cladding** 10 off 1778 × 121 × 12 mm (70 × 4¾ × ½ in) ship lapboarding

**Sill** 1 off 1619 × 86 × 22 mm (63¾ × 3⅜ × ⅞ in) timber

### ROOF

**Stringers** 6 off 3975 × 47 × 47 mm (156½ × 1⅞ × 1⅞ in) timber

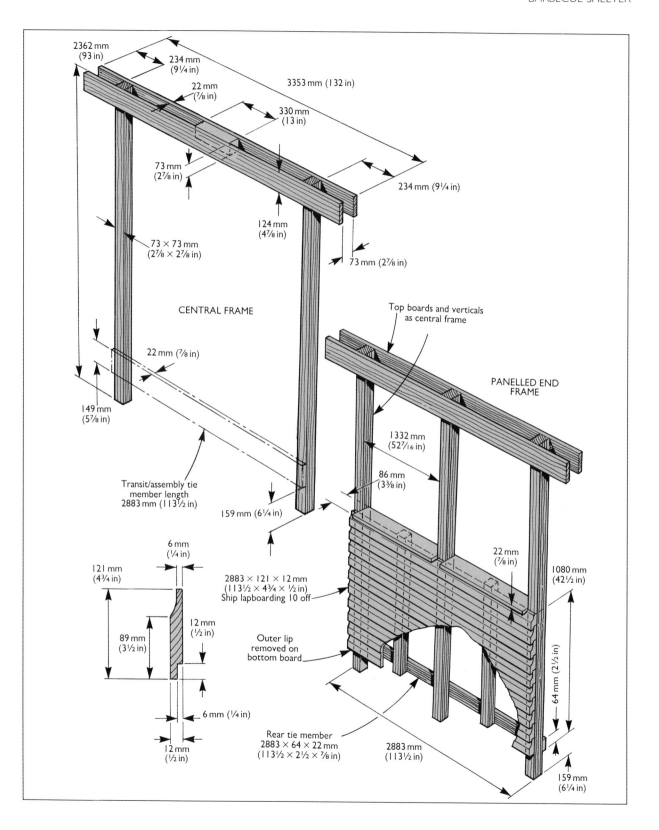

2362 mm
(93 in)

234 mm
(9¼ in)

22 mm
(⅞ in)

3353 mm (132 in)

330 mm
(13 in)

234 mm (9¼ in)

73 mm
(2⅞ in)

124 mm
(4⅞ in)

73 × 73 mm
(2⅞ × 2⅞ in)

73 mm (2⅞ in)

CENTRAL FRAME

22 mm (⅞ in)

149 mm
(5⅞ in)

Transit/assembly tie
member length
2883 mm (113½ in)

159 mm (6¼ in)

Top boards and verticals
as central frame

PANELLED END
FRAME

1332 mm
(52⁷⁄₁₆ in)

86 mm
(3⅜ in)

22 mm
(⅞ in)

1080 mm
(42½ in)

6 mm
(¼ in)

121 mm
(4¾ in)

2883 × 121 × 12 mm
(113½ × 4¾ × ½ in)
Ship lapboarding 10 off

89 mm
(3½ in)

12 mm
(½ in)

64 mm (2½ in)

Outer lip
removed on
bottom board

6 mm (¼ in)

12 mm
(½ in)

Rear tie member
2883 × 64 × 22 mm
(113½ × 2½ × ⅞ in)

2883 mm
(113½ in)

159 mm
(6¼ in)

15

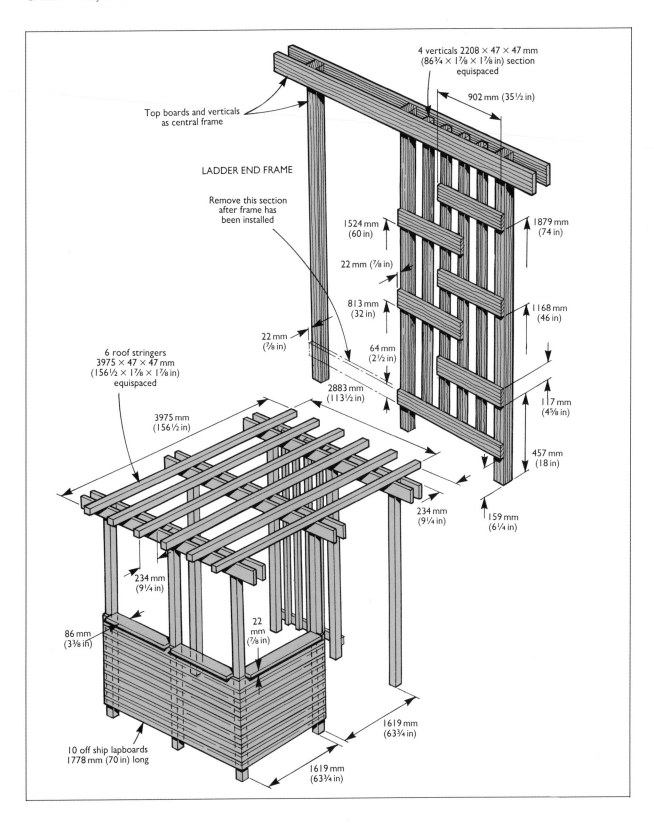

4 verticals 2208 × 47 × 47 mm
(86¾ × 1⅞ × 1⅞ in) section
equispaced

902 mm (35½ in)

Top boards and verticals
as central frame

LADDER END FRAME

Remove this section
after frame has
been installed

1524 mm
(60 in)

22 mm (⅞ in)

813 mm
(32 in)

1879 mm
(74 in)

1168 mm
(46 in)

22 mm
(⅞ in)

64 mm
(2½ in)

2883 mm
(113½ in)

117 mm
(4⅝ in)

457 mm
(18 in)

6 roof stringers
3975 × 47 × 47 mm
(156½ × 1⅞ × 1⅞ in)
equispaced

3975 mm
(156½ in)

234 mm
(9¼ in)

159 mm
(6¼ in)

234 mm
(9¼ in)

22
mm
(⅞ in)

86 mm
(3⅜ in)

1619 mm
(63¾ in)

10 off ship lapboards
1778 mm (70 in) long

1619 mm
(63¾ in)

**5** Now complete the second three-post frame in exactly the same fashion (Step 3–4).

The third, middle, frame is even simpler – it has only two posts, one at each end – but relies even more strongly on a light batten fixed temporarily across the bottom to hold it all square.

Complete all three frames.

**6** The frames really are frames. All three will be covered by wood in one way or another. The three-post frame that is to present itself to the prevailing wind will have a fairly solid surface, made of a type of boarding known as ship lapboarding. Ship lapboard is available from most woodyards, and is a board that allows one piece to interlock with the next, so forming a windproof, waterproof wall.

Nail the lapboard on to the outside of the frame, and saw off any overlapping ends at the edges. This frame will be by far the heaviest of the three when the time comes for removing them to the final site.

Lapboard also features on the smaller middle frame, from one end to the windiest corner of the larger lapboard-covered frame.

The third frame – the second larger frame, with three upright posts – is altogether more decorative, although how it becomes so is up to

**The top of one of the main vertical posts showing timbers screwed on either side. Holding the three frameworks together at the top are six battens of timber (stringers).**

you. There are many ways in which to decorate this side. What I have done is to put up a set of vertical posts between which I have fixed random lengths of horizontal boarding. But battens can be used to make any sort of lattice shape – a diamond pattern can be pleasant to look at, for example.

## SETTING THE SHELTER INTO THE GROUND

**7** Using steel spiked sockets is an ideal way to sink wooden posts into the ground, and helps to avert the rotting to which posts in concrete or hardcore are always doomed. Even so, the ends of the posts should be soaked in a good wood preservative before being put in their sockets. A good method to coat the posts is to stand them up in old paint cans and pour in the preservative, leaving them there for 48 hours or more.

Mark out the position on the ground where the posts are to go, making sure that there are no electricity, gas, drainage, or communications lines beneath. And drive the sockets into the ground using a sledgehammer and the special "driving tool" made by the socket manufacturers for the purpose – anything else may distort the socket edges. Again, for this you will need the assistance of another pair of hands. In clay soil this is an easy job, but in stony ground it is more difficult and frequent checks should be made to ensure that the socket is upright in both planes. If necessary straighten each socket as it goes into the ground by striking the driving tool from one side.

**8** Before you try to place the posts in their sockets, it is best to cut small grooves at the bottom of each post to accommodate the barbs inside each socket. These barbs are intended to grip the post as it enters the socket, therefore don't make your grooves too deep or too wide.

You will have to ask your family and perhaps the neighbours as well to help you set up the completed frames in the sockets in the ground. You may even need a couple of people up stepladders before all three frames are satisfactorily in their places.

You can now unscrew and remove the battens fixed temporarily across the bottom of each frame.

The secret of easy post fixing is to use steel-spiked sockets. A "driving tool" prevents damage to the socket top.

Do not worry if the frames seem to bend towards the top. When battens (stringers) have been screwed across the top, connecting all three frames, the construction will become very rigid. If the posts actually seem loose in their sockets, there is still no need to worry unduly: wood wedges can be driven in at the sockets to firm things up.

**9** The battens that are fitted at the top across the three frames must be positioned and screwed in place with care – which is potentially quite difficult at that height. You will need an angled stepladder on which you can stand quite comfortably and safely, held at the base by an assistant all the time you are working.

**10** Only now is it time to fix the last area of ship lapboarding into one corner of the middle frame to act as a windbreak.

FINISHING OFF

Apply a wood preservative of good quality all over the construction above ground – and give it three coats.

If you want to attach clear corrugated sheet perspex to the roof, remember again to use the stepladder with care (and assistance), to use the special galvanized screws, cups and cap washers that go with such sheets, and to fix the screws and caps on the *tops* of the corrugations.

A wooden half-log border roll is used to create a border around the edges of the Barbecue Shelter.

# BARBECUE CHAIR

THIS TWO-PIECE WOODEN CHAIR IS EASY AND FUN TO MAKE. IT
IS IDEAL FOR USE IN THE BARBECUE SHELTER. WHEN THE
SUMMER IS OVER IT CAN SIMPLY BE DISMANTLED, AND BOTH
PIECES CAN BE HUNG UP ON A HOOK ON THE GARAGE WALL.

Y ou can follow one or other of my alternative designs here from start to finish if
you like, or you may prefer to choose any of a
variety of different styles and patterns of your
own devising, using my designs simply as a basis.

One thing that is essential, though, is that the
wood you choose – and particularly the section
that comprises the actual seat – is completely
free of knots. A knot represents a possible
weak point, and weakness could cause the chair
to break when someone is sitting on it.

### STARTING OUT

**I** First, study the diagrams, and ensure that the
wood you are using is completely knot free, and
that you have all the materials and tools listed.
Carefully mark in pencil the pieces to be cut,
then double-check all dimensions.

**2** Now cut out the shapes. You could do this
with a coping saw, although it would then take
quite a time. It is far quicker to use an electric
jigsaw.

Clamp the wood down firmly before begin-
ning to cut. The best bit to cut first is the long leg
part of the actual seat element.

**3** The back of the chair has two pierced areas
that must be cut out. One is a slot that accom-

The construction of these Barbecue Chairs is
extremely simple – just two pieces of timber are
slotted together.

## MATERIALS

Wood:
two planks
(Candle-wax)
(see Cutting List)

modates the long leg part of the seat. The other provides an easy handhold at the top (although an alternative is to drill some large holes as simple decoration instead).

The easiest method to cut out the pierced areas is again with a jigsaw. Drill a fair-sized hole in both areas, through the hole insert the jigsaw blade, and proceed to cut from there.

### ASSEMBLING THE PARTS

**4** Fitting the long leg part of the seat through the slot in the back may be tricky. It is meant to be a tight fit. But if it really is impossibly tight, matters may be made easier by using a smoothing plane to shave off part of the long leg's thickness. Some candle-wax smeared on the inside edges of the slot may also make the whole thing come together more enthusiastically.

### FINISHING OFF

All the corners and sharp edges of the chair should be rounded off with glasspaper.

The shaping detail at the top of the chair backs can be to your own choice.

### BARBECUE CHAIR CUTTING LIST

**Back** I off 1067 × 222 × 22 mm (42 × 8¾ × ⅞ in) timber
**Seat** I off 1067 × 222 × 22 mm (42 × 8¾ × ⅞ in) timber

The only joint is an elongated slot in the back of the Barbecue Chair that is cut out using a jigsaw. The "tongue" that fits the slot, and comprises the leg of the chair, is also shaped with a jigsaw or a handsaw.

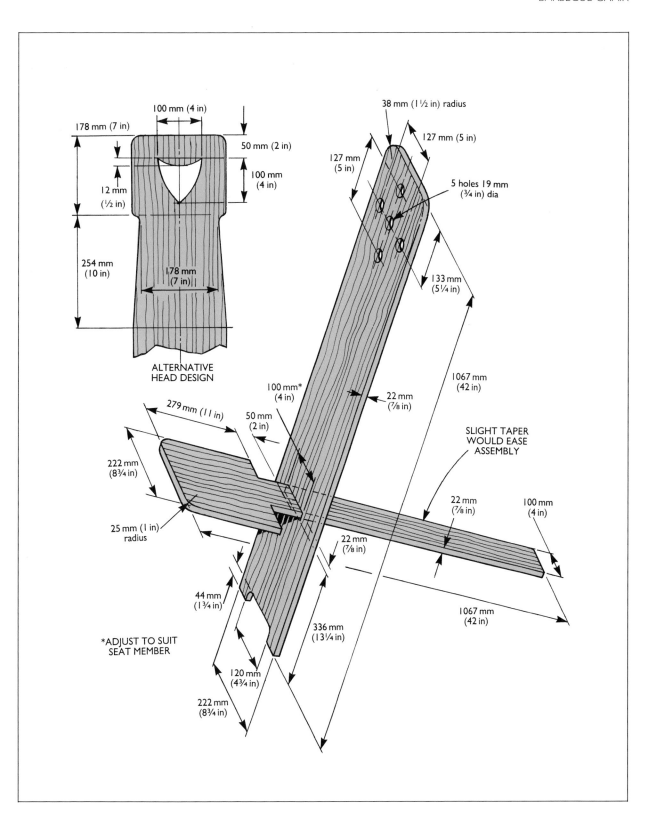

100 mm (4 in)

178 mm (7 in)

50 mm (2 in)

12 mm (½ in)

100 mm (4 in)

254 mm (10 in)

178 mm (7 in)

ALTERNATIVE
HEAD DESIGN

38 mm (1½ in) radius

127 mm (5 in)

127 mm (5 in)

5 holes 19 mm (¾ in) dia

133 mm (5¼ in)

1067 mm (42 in)

SLIGHT TAPER
WOULD EASE
ASSEMBLY

22 mm (⅞ in)

100 mm (4 in)

279 mm (11 in)

100 mm* (4 in)

50 mm (2 in)

22 mm (⅞ in)

222 mm (8¾ in)

25 mm (1 in) radius

22 mm (⅞ in)

22 mm (⅞ in)

1067 mm (42 in)

44 mm (1¾ in)

336 mm (13¼ in)

*ADJUST TO SUIT
SEAT MEMBER

120 mm (4¾ in)

222 mm (8¾ in)

# TABLE AND BENCHES

ANYONE – TRULY ANYONE – CAN MAKE THIS GARDEN TABLE
WITH BENCHES: ALL IT TAKES IS CUTTING THE WOOD
ACCURATELY TO LENGTH AND SCREWING IT TOGETHER.

This is a project that at first sight might look as if it was going to require rather more in the way of tools and time than even a practised amateur woodworker is going to be able to bring to bear. Nonetheless, this is once more a design that requires no traditional jointing skills and yet is constructed for strength and longevity. A competent beginner who has still to attain real confidence can leave out all the twiddles – the non-essential more decorative elements (the curved rails, and so forth) – and regard the project as one that needs only the screwing together of lengths of wood, no more and no less.

I am indebted to Peter Grimsdale for technical skills applied in the basic design.

## STARTING OUT

**1** First study the diagrams. You should have a good idea of what you are going to need even before you buy your wood.

**2** It is even more essential with this project than with some of the other projects that the wood to be used is of the right sort. To this end, a primary step has to be taken at the woodyard, selecting the wood. I recommend Nordic red- or whitewood. But it must be quite straight, without twists. Planks should be tested before purchase by peering down their lengths with one eye, the other eye closed, to look for telltale twists. If the form of a plank bears any kind of resemblance to the crinkly coastline of

its Scandinavian origins, it should be instantly and firmly rejected – or, if there is any sign of remonstration from the woodyard foreman, you could offer to buy it at a nominal price for use as firewood! (That may depend on how excitable he looks, perhaps.) You are the customer: get what you want; be satisfied with nothing else.

**3** Note that in this design the legs and the side rails are really all one unit: the legs of the benches and the table are each trapped between two horizontal rails at the bottom.

Carefully mark with a pencil on the four horizontal rails (feet) exactly where the bench and table legs are to be positioned. The best method is to mark all four rails at once: use a genuinely flat surface to lay them on, and a pair of G-clamps to hold them firmly together while being marked. And to make sure that the lines are correctly perpendicular, use a carpenter's square to mark across the tops of the four rails.

**4** Now mark out and cut to length the four table legs and eight bench legs. Be sure to cut the ends off squarely (or you will have difficulty later in fitting on the bench and table tops).

A good ordinary handsaw is quite sufficient for the job – but I have to recommend the use of a hand-held electric circular saw, especially

**This Table and Benches will enhance any garden. No problems with traditional joints, just cut the timber accurately to length then glue and screw it together.**

## MATERIALS

Wood:

   planks

   rails/battens

   posts (for legs)

Zinc-plated Supascrews

Wood preservative

(see Cutting List)

one with a safety button (so that both hands are occupied and out of the way) and preferably with a tungsten carbide blade (which cuts more cleanly than steel and stays sharp for longer).

## ASSEMBLING THE PARTS

**5** Next, take two table legs and four bench legs, and position them between two horizontal rails. Clamp the two rails together with a G-clamp at both ends, and use a carpenter's square to position the legs exactly against the pencil lines already marked, vertically and horizontally – the legs must be at right-angles to the horizontal rails.

When the legs are securely in place, drill pilot holes for the screws – four through each leg – through the horizontal rails, using a small drill. (If you do not drill pilot holes, there is the chance that with such large screws you will not be physically able to drive them home, or that the heads will shear off long before.) Finish off each pilot hole with a counterboring bit at the outer edge so that the heads of the screws when driven in will be below the wood surface. Then drive the twin-threaded zinc-plated Supascrews through the pilot holes, so that each one

passes through a horizontal rail, a leg, and the farther horizontal rail, and its head comes to rest below the wood surface.

Again, an ordinary hand screwdriver is perfectly adequate for the job, only in this case the job will be fairly strenuous and time-consuming – so I recommend the use of a battery-powered electric screwdriver/drill. It really does simplify matters; it certainly speeds things up. Many amateurs have found they are able to tackle jobs they had previously thought unmanageable by coming into possession of one of these remarkably useful tools.

Now repeat the whole of Step 5 with the other legs and the remaining two horizontal

## USEFUL TIP

Tungsten-tipped circular saw blades last much longer and are essential for cutting man-made boards.

Use a hand-held circular saw to cut the legs to width. There are many such cutting operations throughout the book, and having the ability to cut them yourself is a great time and money saver.

## TABLE AND BENCHES CUTTING LIST

**Feet** 4 off 1524 × 149 × 22 mm (60 × 5⅞ × ⅞ in) timber

**Bench supports** 8 off 432 × 149 × 22 mm (17 × 5⅞ × ⅞ in) timber

**Outer bench stiffener** 2 off 1175 × 149 × 22 mm (46¼ × 5⅞ × ⅞ in) timber

**Inner bench stiffener** 2 off 1175 × 44 × 22 mm (46¼ × 1¾ × ⅞ in) timber

**Bench central cross-tie** 2 off 248 × 44 × 22 mm (9¾ × 1¾ × ⅞ in) timber

**Bench top** 4 off 1524 × 149 × 22 mm (60 × 5⅞ × ⅞ in) timber

**Table legs** 4 off 762 × 149 × 22 mm (30 × 5⅞ × ⅞ in) timber

**Table cross-rail** 1 off 1435 × 149 × 22 mm (56½ × 5⅞ × ⅞ in) timber

**Wedge** 2 off 229 × 44 × 22 mm (9 × 1¾ × ⅞ in) timber

**Table-top side rail** 2 off 610 × 149 × 22 mm (24 × 5⅞ × ⅞ in) timber

**Table-top length rail** 2 off 1220 × 102 × 22 mm (48 × 4 × ⅞ in) timber

**Table-top cross-piece** 1 off 565 × 102 × 22 mm (22¼ × 4 × ⅞ in) timber

**Table-top slats** 4 off 1524 × 149 × 22 mm (60 × 5⅞ × ⅞ in) timber

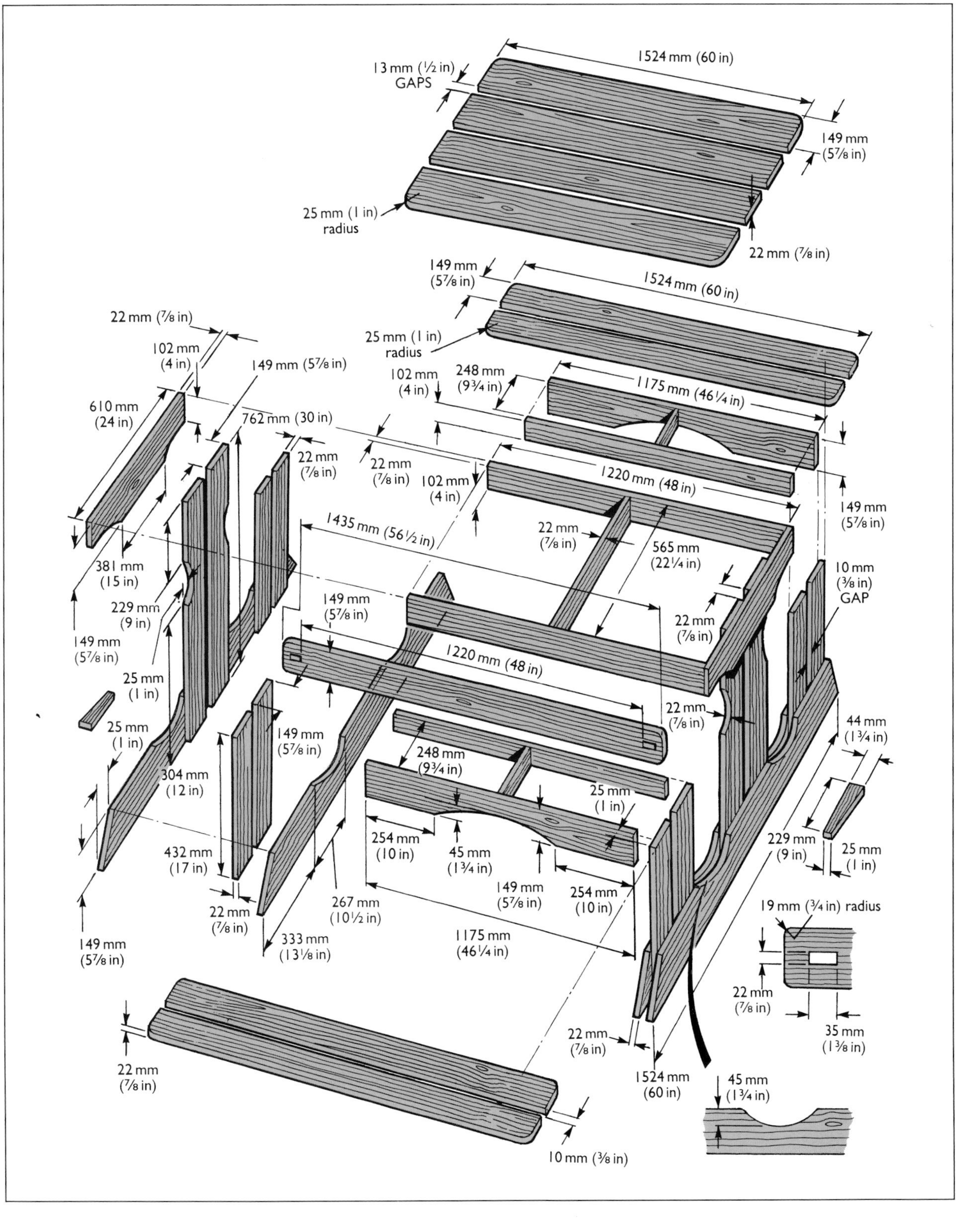
1524 mm (60 in)
13 mm (½ in) GAPS
149 mm (5⅞ in)
25 mm (1 in) radius
22 mm (⅞ in)
149 mm (5⅞ in)
1524 mm (60 in)
22 mm (⅞ in)
25 mm (1 in) radius
102 mm (4 in)
149 mm (5⅞ in)
102 mm (4 in)
248 mm (9¾ in)
1175 mm (46¼ in)
610 mm (24 in)
762 mm (30 in)
22 mm (⅞ in)
22 mm (⅞ in)
102 mm (4 in)
1220 mm (48 in)
149 mm (5⅞ in)
1435 mm (56½ in)
22 mm (⅞ in)
565 mm (22¼ in)
381 mm (15 in)
10 mm (⅜ in) GAP
229 mm (9 in)
149 mm (5⅞ in)
22 mm (⅞ in)
149 mm (5⅞ in)
1220 mm (48 in)
25 mm (1 in)
22 mm (⅞ in)
25 mm (1 in)
149 mm (5⅞ in)
44 mm (1¾ in)
248 mm (9¾ in)
304 mm (12 in)
25 mm (1 in)
229 mm (9 in)
25 mm (1 in)
432 mm (17 in)
254 mm (10 in)
45 mm (1¾ in)
149 mm (5⅞ in)
254 mm (10 in)
22 mm (⅞ in)
267 mm (10½ in)
19 mm (¾ in) radius
149 mm (5⅞ in)
333 mm (13⅛ in)
1175 mm (46¼ in)
22 mm (⅞ in)
35 mm (1⅜ in)
22 mm (⅞ in)
22 mm (⅞ in)
1524 mm (60 in)
45 mm (1¾ in)
10 mm (⅜ in)

rails. You should finally have two identical ends, each of which has six pieces of wood sticking out from them!

**6** Take one end assembly and attach a table-top side rail to the pair of table legs such that the rail overlaps the top edge of each leg by 3 mm (⅛ in). With the rail clamped in position, drill pilot holes through it into each leg, counterbore the pilot holes, and screw the rail to the legs.

The reason for the overlap is that the end grain of the legs is likely to expand: the overlap gives it room to do so without affecting any other part of the construction.

Repeat Step 6 with the other end.

**7** This is an optional Step, and depends on how confident you are. It comprises cutting the curved shapes on the table legs, the bottom rails and the top table rail in the way you can see in the photographs. To do it I used a jigsaw. Good, isn't it?

But if you feel your construction is beautiful

The feet at the bottom of the table are shaped with a jigsaw to allow for ease of entry and exit.

enough without needless luxuries, go straight on to Step 8.

**8** Now the two ends have to be fixed together. For this purpose I have used a length of wood that fits between the two table legs and is a main structural component, adding stability to the entire construction. The traditional method of fixing such a rail was with a large wedge at each end, held hard against the outside of the legs – a custom I like in my tables too: wedges look good and are practical.

Set the rail between the table legs and mark with a pencil where the outside edges of the legs come. Remove the rail and in pencil complete the square that has to be cut out to accommodate the wedge. To cut out the square, the easiest method is to bore a large hole and then use a sharp chisel to expand the corners out to the square.

Wedges can be cut from spare pieces of wood. Chamfer off the thin ends of the wedges to prevent the edges from splitting. (Do not drive in the wedges yet: just assemble them in place.)

**9** Now cut the rails on which the top of the table will rest. Cut to length, the rails are set in position, pilot holes are drilled (and counterbored), waterproof glue is coated on adjoining surfaces, and screws are finally driven in. A cross-piece is fitted half-way along the table top, similarly glued and screwed into each of these side rails, and forming an excellent structural bar to which the table-top planks can in turn be screwed down.

At all times check for squareness.

**10** Rails are now fitted to connect the legs of the benches. (At this stage there is once more the option of cutting curves in the rails if desired.) The rails are set in position, against the inside edges of the legs, pilot holes are drilled (and counterbored), and the screws finally driven home.

At all times check for squareness.

**11** Check over the whole structure to make totally sure that it is all square – that the right-

wooden plugs to fill the counterbore holes above the screw heads, glue them, and hammer them tightly home: this gives a nice clean finish to important surfaces.

When the glue has cured (set), use a sharp chisel to take off any excess plug top, and glasspaper over all the planks, sides, rails and edges. There must be no sharp projections on which legs or hands may be damaged.

FINISHING OFF
Finally, drive the wedges in tight.

It is essential that the whole construction is treated with a good wood preservative.

Cutting a wedge hole for the Garden Table. The table has a horizontal bar running full length between the legs. The hole for each wedge is chopped out using a chisel and mallet.

angles are indeed all of ninety degrees. Not until this stage does the whole construction begin to take on its final rigidity, and hereafter it may weaken the structure to have to make alterations to take account of unnecessary errors.

**12** Before positioning the planks that form the table top and the bench seats, they have to be shaped. Round off all the corners with a smoothing plane, and gently chamfer all the inside and outside edges.

They can then be glued and screwed down. Drill pilot holes, counterbore to some depth, coat adjoining sides with waterproof glue, and drive in the screws. Using a plug cutter, make

The screws that hold the table and bench tops in place are hidden by wooden plugs. The holes are counterbored, the screw is inserted and a wooden plug is glued over the top and then trimmed flush using a sharp chisel.

# TWO-SEATER BENCH

OF ALL THE PIECES OF GARDEN FURNITURE IN THIS BOOK, THE
GARDEN SEAT WITH ITS CENTRAL TABLE IS MY OWN
FAVOURITE. TO SIT IN THE GARDEN AND HAVE A HANDY PLACE
TO PUT A DRINK DOWN IS A DELIGHT.

The project may seem dauntingly big and rather intricate. But my design avoids all the more complicated traditional joints: jointing is done solely with Supascrews and glue. A look at the construction diagram should reassure you that the whole thing is made up simply of lengths of wood cut to size and shape, and glued and screwed together.

Some of the pieces of wood needed in this Project are relatively large: make sure you have a working area that is both big enough and flat – a garage floor, or driveway, perhaps. The range of tools required is also a little larger than for other projects: above all you will need a sharp handsaw and a screwdriver with an undamaged driving end (as opposed to one that has been used for opening cans of paint).

You can simplify my design if you wish – there is no real need to shape the backrests of the seats or the front of the table, for example. I also prefer to use a plug cutter and make wooden plugs to cover over the counterbored screw heads – but not to use plugs is unimportant from a structural point of view and can save a great deal of time.

Selection of the wood to be used is critical. Choose wood that is square at the edges, that is flat, and that has no twists. Above all, ensure that it is clean and dry – wet wood is of no use to anybody – and do not be panicked into purchases by a smooth-talking assistant. In wood to

be used for the underframe and the legs, avoid any that has knots and try to stick to the dimensions I recommend as closely as possible. (I did design this Project thinking to myself that if a hippo came to tea the bench would take the strain – but any real reduction in the dimensions of these particular elements would compromise the structure's overall strength.)

## BASE ASSEMBLY

**1** First study the drawings. Try to get the cutting list memorized, especially if you have not yet purchased your wood – that way, if you see wood offered at a discount price you will know immediately if it is suitable for your purposes. Once all the wood is in your working area, carefully mark in pencil all the pieces to be cut, checking the dimensions before and after to be certain, and always remembering to allow for the thickness of the saw cut itself.

Begin by cutting to length the back and front struts of the underframe: they must be absolutely identical. Now cut the side pieces of the frame: they too must be precisely identical in length.

**2** The underframe should now be glued and screwed together. Check once more that the

It's hard to beat the traditional garden bench for a comfortable sit. However, with the addition of a table in the middle to hold the drinks, what could be more restful?

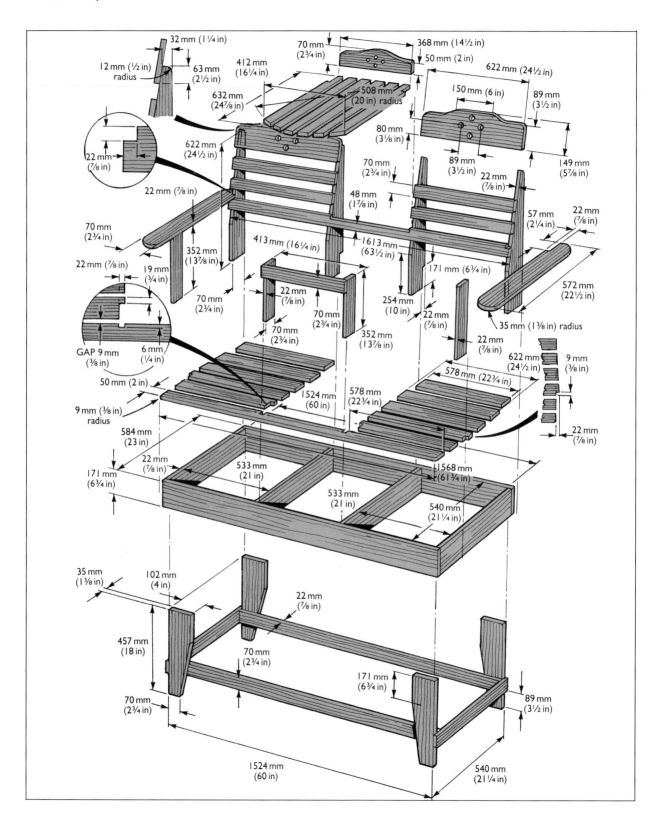

front and back, and the two sides, are identical pairs in terms of length.

*Method:* At both ends of the front and back, drill holes to take fairly large zinc-plated screws – No. 8, 5 cm (2 in) long, say. Countersink the screw holes and, if you mean to use wood plugs to conceal the screw heads, use a plug cutter to make plugs to fit the counterbored holes.

Drill all the holes. Then, one corner at a time, glue the surfaces that are to be joined and drive the screws in tightly. You may well need a sash cramp (or an extra pair of hands) to help hold things together.

When all four corners have been glued and screwed – and before the glue cures (sets) – check the resulting solid framework for squareness. The best way to do this is to place a long batten across the frame from one corner to the diagonally opposite corner, and mark where the corners fall on the batten. Now place the batten across the other two diagonal corners and see if the marks tally as they should. If they don't, gently press against one end corner until the same test proves that the frame is correctly squared up. Check also that the frame is absolutely flat, and is positioned on a flat surface. (The best way to do this is to see how it lies on a large sheet of thick, flat plywood.)

If the frame is square and flat, give the glue time to cure.

**3** Two further struts of wood are now glued and screwed into the underframe in similar

## MATERIALS

Wood:
  planks
  battens
  posts (for legs and
    supports)
Zinc-plated Supascrews
Twin-threaded long
  Supascrews
Wood preservative
(Varnish/paint)
(see Cutting List)

## TWO-SEATER BENCH CUTTING LIST

**BASE ASSEMBLY**

**Longitudinal struts** 2 off 1524 × 171 × 22 mm (60 × 6¾ × ⅞ in) timber

**Sides** 2 off 584 × 171 × 22 mm (23 × 6¾ × ⅞ in) timber

**Intermediates** 2 off 540 × 171 × 22 mm (21¼ × 6¾ × ⅞ in) timber

**LEG ASSEMBLY**

**Legs** 4 off 457 × 102 × 35 mm (18 × 4 × 1⅜ in) timber

**Longitudinal rail** 2 off 1524 × 70 × 22 mm (60 × 2¾ × ⅞ in) timber

**Side rails** 2 off 540 × 70 × 22 mm (21¼ × 2¾ × ⅞ in) timber

**TABLE FRAME**

**Rear supports** 2 off 622 × 70 × 22 mm (24½ × 2¾ × ⅞ in) timber

**Front supports** 2 off 352 × 70 × 22 mm (13⅞ × 2¾ × ⅞ in) timber

**Front rail** 1 off 413 × 70 × 22 mm (16¼ × 2¾ × ⅞ in) timber

**ARMS AND SUPPORTS**

**Arms** 2 off 572 × 70 × 22 mm (22½ × 2¾ × ⅞ in) timber

**Backrest struts** 4 off 622 × 70 × 22 mm (24½ × 2¾ × ⅞ in) timber

**Armrest supports** 2 off 352 × 70 × 22 mm (13⅞ × 2¾ × ⅞ in) timber

**SEAT ASSEMBLY**

**Front slat** 1 off 1568 × 51 × 22mm (61¾ × 2 × ⅞ in) timber

**Second slat** 2 off 600 × 70 × 22 mm (23⅝ × 2¾ × ⅞ in) timber

**Third to sixth slats** 8 off 622 × 70 × 22 mm (24½ × 2¾ × ⅞ in) timber

**Seventh slat** 2 off 578 × 70 × 22 mm (22¾ × 2¾ × ⅞ in) timber

**TABLE TOP ASSEMBLY**

**Slats** 6 off 632 × 64 × 22 mm (24⅞ × 2½ × ⅞ in) timber

**Rear vertical** 1 off 368 × 70 × 22mm (14½ × 2¾ × ⅞ in) timber

**SEAT BACK ASSEMBLY**

**Full-length slat** 1 off 1613 × 70 × 22 mm (63½ × 2¾ × ⅞ in) timber

**Intermediates** 4 off 622 × 70 × 22 mm (24½ × 2¾ × ⅞ in) timber

**Headboard** 2 off 622 × 149 × 22 mm (24½ × 5⅞ × ⅞ in) timber

fashion. They are to provide the support for the seat centre sections and for the table. While the glue is still wet, check that they too are both square and flat with the rest of the frame.

## LEG ASSEMBLY

**4** Now it is time to cut and shape the legs. Cutting a taper on the lengths is not difficult but does essentially require that the wood is firmly clamped while being sawn. (Theoretically, timber is never difficult to cut, it is holding it steady that presents the problems.) A useful tip in these circumstances is to cut the legs longer than necessary: this gives an additional length at top or bottom for holding in a vice or clamp. Wasteful this idea may be – but it saves fingers!

Remove the roughness of the saw cuts using a smoothing plane.

**5** The next task is to glue and screw the legs into the inside corners of the underframe. Drill pilot holes for all the screws through the legs and into the frame. (Without pilot holes the screws may shear off or the wood may split.) Then glue and screw on the legs one at a time.

**6** To lend rigidity to the legs, a rail is attached between them. The rail at the front is fixed at the back of the legs. This allows the line or taper

of the legs to show clearly (and looks better). The rail at the sides is glued and screwed to the outer edge of the legs.

**7** To avoid the possibility of splitting or splintering the wood of a leg when the whole table is pulled along the ground (as may well happen in the garden or on a patio), it is wise to take the precaution of cutting small chamfers around all four sides of the foot of each leg. Use a chisel or a plane.

## ARMS AND SUPPORTS

**8** Now for the assembly of the four backrest struts and the two armrest supports. These pieces would traditionally have been combined with the structure of the legs, but my design is no less in strength and attractiveness, and avoids some of the difficulties posed by such traditional features.

Like the legs, the backrest struts have to be cut to a taper (see Step 4). When they are cut, remove the rough saw marks by using a sharp plane. Then glue and screw the backrest struts to the back of the frame. The best method for doing this is to screw on the two end struts first, clamp a length of batten temporarily across the top of them, and line up the middle two struts against the batten while screwing them in.

Fix the armrest supports as shown in the diagram.

## TABLE AND SEAT ASSEMBLY

**9** Now cut and fit the two front table leg supports. Glue and screw them to the front inside edges of the frame.

At the back, prepare a batten to fit on to the backrest struts. You will have to plane a slight angle on the top of this batten to offset the angle on the backrest struts.

**10** The next task is to cut the seat and table slats. The exact dimensions of slat I have suggested may not be available from your wood supplier. The width of slat is not vitally significant, however, provided you keep a consistent distance between slats.

---

### USEFUL TIP

Battery powered screwdriver/drills enhance the scope of the woodworker – screws are driven into the wood so easily. It's true to say that once you have used one you wonder how you ever managed without it.

Drilling the pilot holes for the leg assembly, using a battery powered screwdriver.

All the slats used on the seats and table have chamfered edges. Use a smoothing plane to remove sharp edges, before the battens are attached, and finish off with glasspaper.

It is important to fit the table supports before fitting the table slats, because some of the slats have to have square notches removed to accommodate the supports. Mark them out carefully and label them in pencil so they (and you) do not get confused.

The seat slats have all sharp edges planed off: I find that four to five passes with a smoothing plane is just about sufficient. Then finish off by rubbing down with glasspaper. Drill pilot holes for fixing all the slats to the frame. Some of these slats too will have to have notches cut from them to fit around the legs.

II In cutting and shaping the armrests it is important to round off the front edges and to remove the sharp corners from the sides. Cut a small notch out of the back of the armrest to fit around the backrest support. The cut has to be

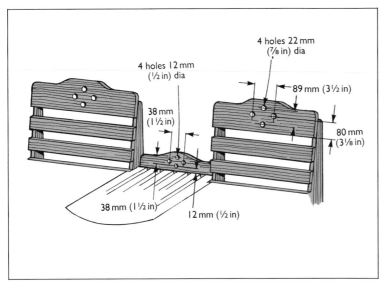

4 holes 22 mm
(⁷⁄₈ in) dia

4 holes 12 mm
(½ in) dia

89 mm (3½ in)

38 mm
(1½ in)

80 mm
(3⅛ in)

38 mm (1½ in)

12 mm (½ in)

**These holes are bored simply as a form of decoration. You may wish to experiment with larger holes; or, using a jigsaw, heart-shaped motifs can be cut out.**

at a slight angle in order to accommodate the angle on the backrest support. The armrest is secured at the back by driving two screws through the backrest strut into the armrest. At the front, the armrest is fixed to its support by two long screws that pass from the top of the armrest through into the endgrain of the

support: the length is important to ensure that a good fixing is made into the endgrain. (I can recommend the twin-threaded Supascrew for this application.)

**12** The slats that form the backrest itself have now to be shaped. Cut them to length, and once again plane of all the sharp edges, and finish with glasspaper.

The top of the seat has rather more elaborately ornate boarding comprising wider planks of wood. Drill decorative holes in the appropriate places. The shaping of the top edge can be cut with a coping saw or a jigsaw. All edges should be glasspapered smooth.

**13** Now cut the table slats to length. To give a little shaping to the table, lay out all the slats in position; then, using a pencil on a string attached to the central slat at the back, scribe a segment of a circle across the top ends of the slats. Working to the pencil line, then use a jigsaw to cut the curve across the slats. Before fixing, plane off all the sharp edges.

**14** For decorative purposes only, a small piece of wood should be shaped to fit on the back of the table, just like the tops of the seats (see Step 11). As there, drill decorative holes, only in this case use a smaller bit to remain in scale.

### FINISHING OFF

If, throughout this construction, you have been intending to use wood plugs to conceal all the screw heads, and have been using a counterbore bit for that reason, now is the time to plug all the holes.

Cut the plugs with a plug cutter, and glue them in place. It may be that the shortgrain causes a plug to snap off below the level of the slat surface: in that case, dig out the broken plug with a sharp point and replace it with a new one. Once the glue has cured, pare off any extra wood or waste glue with a sharp chisel, leaving an almost invisible joint.

A complete coating of good weatherproof paint, varnish, or wood preservative is essential before the bench begins life in the garden.

# GARDEN BRIDGE

A BRIDGE CAN MAKE A MOST UNUSUAL – AND VERY ENJOYABLE – FEATURE IN YOUR GARDEN.

People have more time, today, not only to work in their gardens but to sit in them. Many have added new features, such as ponds and streams. There may even be trickling cascades or splashing waterfalls. So why not a bridge? A bridge does not have to span the pond or stream: it can connect one part of a garden to another – from the garden path to the rockery, for instance.

The bridge as illustrated may look perhaps rather complex, but in reality it is not difficult to build. And as usual with my construction, there are no awkward, old-fashioned joints to have to fit together: it is simply a matter of using Supa-screws, glue, and zinc-plated coach-bolts.

## STARTING OUT

**1** First study the diagram. You should have a good idea of what you are going to need even before you buy your wood.

It is even more essential with this project than with some of the other projects that the wood to be used for the two main side members of the bridge, and for the slats which form the path over it, is of the right sort. Both need to be completely free of knots. Careful personal selection of the wood at the woodyard is essential. Of the many grades of wood available in woodyards, the rather expensive grade known as "joinery quality" is probably the best for this job.

**2** Once the wood is back in your workshop (or garage), the first task is to mark out the curve of the bridge sides. There are many clever ways in which to do this . . . but the simplest is to call on the services of a couple of helpers and a long, thin, pliable but springy batten. With a pencil, mark a line that is to be the centre of the bridge. Then ask the two helpers to bow (bend) the batten by a similar amount at each end, so that the centre of the curved batten aligns with the centre of the bridge side piece. With a bit of experimenting you should be able sooner or later to achieve a good, steady, flowing curve that can then be transferred to the bridge side using a soft pencil run along the batten.

The operation is comparatively simple, even if you and your helpers find yourselves holding your breath for the entire time the batten is being bowed to the requisite degree until the curve is finally marked. Be prepared to make several attempts if necessary. A pencil eraser may well be put to good use in the meantime!

**3** Once the curve has been marked, it is time to cut it out. This is a job for a jigsaw and preferably one with safety features such as a clear plastic guard at the front cutting edge to prevent fingers from ever coming in contact with the blade. Such jigsaws are among the most capable and safe of woodworking machines.

Clamp the wood firmly to a bench or table as you cut along the curved line. Cut with care, for you will be able to use the offcut as a template to mark in the parallel curve at the under edge of the bridge side member.

So, once the first curve is cut, take the offcut, position it at the appropriate distance beneath the first cut and, making sure it is parallel to the

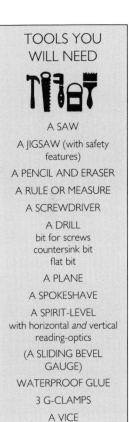

## MATERIALS

Wood:

  knot-free boards of
    "joinery quality" or
    equivalent

  battens/slats (for the
    pathway, the underside,
    and for marking)

  6 posts

  caps for the posts

  panels or lengths of wood
    (for the bridge-ends)

  long, thin, springy batten
    (for measurement and
    marking)

Zinc-plated Supascrews

Zinc-plated coach-bolts,
  large, smaller

Galvanized washers for
  both bolt sizes

Wood preservative

Paint

(see Cutting List)

first cut, pencil in the curve. Before cutting again, check at each end of the curve to make sure once and for all that the line is really parallel. And cut, using the jigsaw.

Now you have a piece of timber curved in parallel at top and bottom, representing one bridge side member.

**4** Fix the side member in a vice or worktable, and use a spokeshave to remove traces of the saw's cutting. The spokeshave is one of those ancient tools that are matchless for their purpose: it removes saw-cut marks rapidly and leaves a super-smooth finish. With the spokeshave always work downwards with the curve, then reverse the wood to work down the curve from the other side – pass the bottom of the curve and you risk tearing the wood. Gently smooth out any high spots with the spokeshave, working carefully with an eye on the desired line.

Once all the curves are smooth and graceful, place the finished bridge side member against the other so-far-unused side member piece, and use it as a template to mark both the curves in with a pencil.

Clamping the piece firmly on both occasions, use the jigsaw to cut out the two curves on the second side member; then use the spokeshave again to smooth out the saw-cuts.

You should at that stage have two identical bridge side members.

### ASSEMBLING THE PARTS

**5** Now glue and screw lengths of wood on to the underside of the bridge: two at each end of the bridge side members. To do this may be a little awkward because the rounded part of the curved section is resting on the ground, but persevere. Drill pilot holes at the ends of each length, and coat with waterproof glue the surfaces that are to be joined. Check for

**Many gardens already have a pond or even a rockery waterfall, and this simple-to-construct foot bridge will add a further dimension to the garden.**

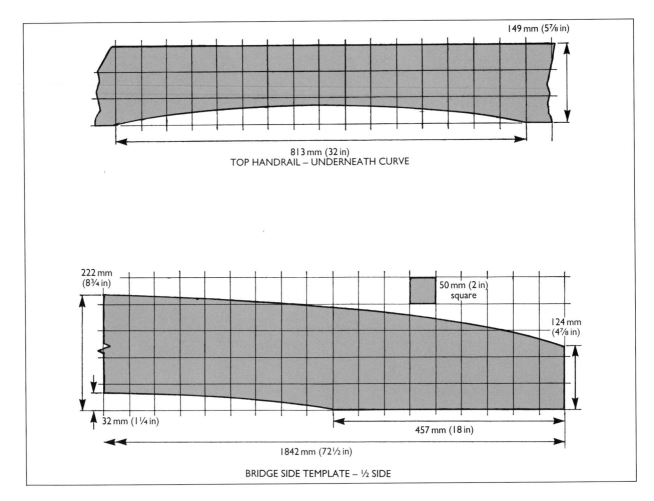

149 mm (5⅞ in)

813 mm (32 in)
TOP HANDRAIL – UNDERNEATH CURVE

222 mm
(8¾ in)

50 mm (2 in)
square

124 mm
(4⅞ in)

32 mm (1¼ in)

457 mm (18 in)

1842 mm (72½ in)

BRIDGE SIDE TEMPLATE – ½ SIDE

straightness as each length of wood is finally screwed down – before the glue cures (sets).

**6** The next task is to cut the battens or slats that are to be the path across the bridge. To save time, the best method is to cut one batten to length, and then to use it as a template to mark up and cut all the other battens. (It is far easier to have all the battens cut to exactly the same length from the first than to try and trim them more precisely at the end of the job.)

## GARDEN BRIDGE CUTTING LIST

**Side member** 2 off 1842 × 222 × 22 mm (72½ × 8¾ × ⅞ in) timber

**Top handrail** 2 off 2388 × 149 × 22 mm (94 × 5⅞ × ⅞ in) timber

**Bottom handrail** 2 off 2160 × 73 × 22 mm (85 × 2⅞ × ⅞ in) timber

**Support posts** 6 off 920 × 73 × 47 mm (36¼ × 2⅞ × 1⅞ in) timber

**Post caps** 4 off 98 × 73 × 22 mm (3⅞ × 2⅞ × ⅞ in) timber
2 off 114 × 73 × 22 mm (4½ × 2⅞ × ⅞ in) timber

**End boards** 2 off 457 × 146 × 22 mm (18 × 5¾ × ⅞ in) timber

**Under cross-pieces** 4 off 457 × 149 × 22 mm (18 × 5⅞ × ⅞ in) timber

**Slats/battens** 31 off 457 × 44 × 22 mm (18 × 1¾ × ⅞ in) timber

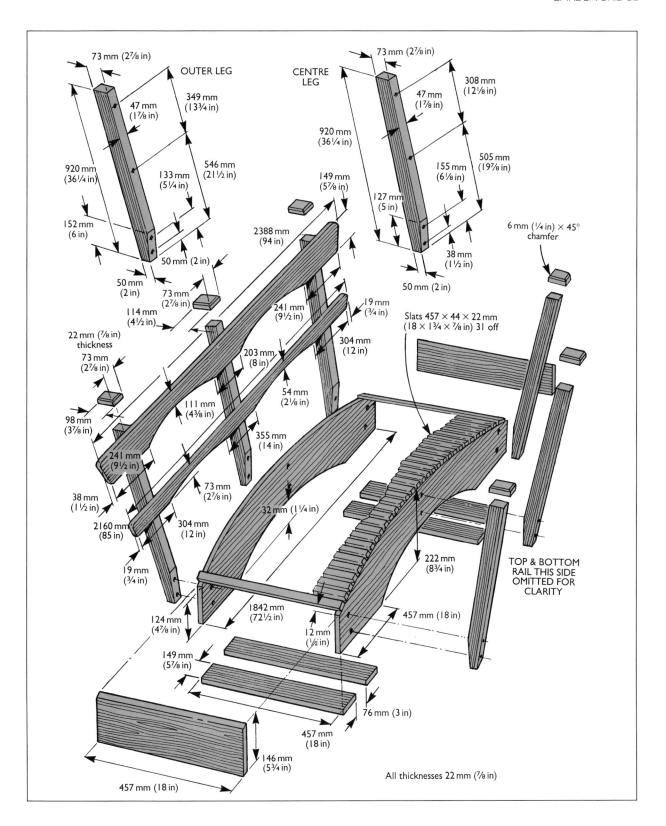

OUTER LEG

CENTRE LEG

73 mm (2⅞ in)

73 mm (2⅞ in)

47 mm (1⅞ in)

349 mm (13¾ in)

308 mm (12⅛ in)

47 mm (1⅞ in)

920 mm (36¼ in)

546 mm (21½ in)

505 mm (19⅞ in)

133 mm (5¼ in)

920 mm (36¼ in)

155 mm (6⅛ in)

127 mm (5 in)

152 mm (6 in)

149 mm (5⅞ in)

6 mm (¼ in) × 45° chamfer

38 mm (1½ in)

2388 mm (94 in)

19 mm (¾ in)

50 mm (2 in)

50 mm (2 in)

50 mm (2 in)

73 mm (2⅞ in)

241 mm (9½ in)

304 mm (12 in)

Slats 457 × 44 × 22 mm (18 × 1¾ × ⅞ in) 31 off

114 mm (4½ in)

203 mm (8 in)

22 mm (⅞ in) thickness

54 mm (2⅛ in)

73 mm (2⅞ in)

111 mm (4⅜ in)

98 mm (3⅞ in)

355 mm (14 in)

241 mm (9½ in)

73 mm (2⅞ in)

38 mm (1½ in)

32 mm (1¼ in)

2160 mm (85 in)

304 mm (12 in)

222 mm (8¾ in)

TOP & BOTTOM RAIL THIS SIDE OMITTED FOR CLARITY

19 mm (¾ in)

124 mm (4⅞ in)

1842 mm (72½ in)

457 mm (18 in)

12 mm (½ in)

149 mm (5⅞ in)

76 mm (3 in)

146 mm (5¾ in)

457 mm (18 in)

457 mm (18 in)

All thicknesses 22 mm (⅞ in)

Planks of timber are screwed to the underside of the bridge, to give both stability and a flat area on which the bridge rests.

Handrail posts are coach-bolted to the sides. The posts are offset, giving a pleasant angle to the handrails.

Now turn the bridge up the right way, and fix the first of the battens on at the centre. Positioning is very easy: the first line you marked in your construction of this Project was the bridge's centre. Glue and screw the batten down, first drilling and countersinking pilot holes at each end and adding a spot of glue on adjoining surfaces. The type of screw I recommend is 3 mm (1/8 in, No. 8) wide and at least 35 mm (1 1/2 in) long. The rest of the slats are also to be glued and screwed, and you may like to drill and countersink the pilot holes for the screws in all of them as a single initial operation.

To keep the interval between successive slats an identical distance when fixing them on, it is a good idea first to plane a length of spare batten to the size and shape of the interval, and to place it up against each slat as it is fixed and to position the next batten against it. This relieves you of the otherwise potentially irksome need to keep measuring the interval distance.

After fixing the first two or three slats in place, check again for squareness.

### THE HANDRAILS AND SUPPORT POSTS

**7** Once all the slats have been fixed in place and the bridge is a solid pathway, turn your attention to the handrails and support posts.

All the posts supporting the handrails are fitted using coach-bolts. Coach-bolts are available in many widths and lengths: the ones I have used to attach the support posts to the bridge are 9 mm (3/8 in) in diameter. Although coach-bolts have a rounded head, the top of the shank immediately beneath the head is square in section; as the nut is screwed on to the bolt, tightening it, it is the square section that by its shape prevents the head from turning round within the hole. Zinc-plated bolts are essential for this Project – they are also cleaner to handle than ordinary coach-bolts – and it is worth making every effort to obtain them.

The bridge's overall appearance is much improved if the handrails slope outwards slightly. To achieve this, an angle has to be planed on to the inside edge at the bottom of each support post. Mark the angle on the posts in pencil. A sliding bevel gauge is useful for this – it is simple to get the gauge to the correct angle and transfer it on to the bottom inside edges of all six posts. Secure each post in a vice and, using a handsaw, cut off the angle. With a plane, carefully smooth right down to the pencil line.

**8** The first post is to be fitted to the middle of the bridge – where, you will remember, the centre line is already marked. A good, large

G-clamp is required to hold the post to the side of the bridge. As you can see in the illustration, each support post is secured by two coach-bolts, for which holes have to be drilled. Use a flat bit to bore a hole just deep enough to take the head of the coach-bolt beneath the surrounding wood surface. The flat bit has a spike at the centre which makes a perfect starting hole for the 9 mm (3/8 in) diameter wood bit that should now be used to bore a hole right through the post and through the side of the bridge. It is important to keep the G-clamp absolutely firm during this operation – and important also not to try to drill the holes independently without a clamp – or there may well be considerable difficulty in aligning the various holes in post and bridge.

The first hole drilled, fit the coach-bolt through it, thread a galvanized washer on the end, and then the nut. Wind the nut down the thread, but at first do it up only lightly. Remove the G-clamp and check that the post is going on vertically: use a spirit-level with a vertical reading-optic. Replace the G-clamp. Drill the second hole in the post and fit the second bolt, lightly again. Remove the G-clamp and check even more closely for verticality. Then tighten up the nuts.

The posts at both ends of the bridge are fitted in exactly the same way. Remember to set them at the outward angle.

**9** The handrails require shaping on the under edge only: the top is straight, and so contrasts appealingly with the general curve of the bridge. The curve for the under edge is marked up in the same way as the curve for the bridge sides was, however, the operation is simpler this time because the curve is smaller.

When the under edges of both handrails have been shaped, use a spokeshave again to smooth off the edges. With the spokeshave then also round off the top edges.

To attach each handrail, temporarily fix it fairly lightly with G-clamps first to the outer supports (at each end of the bridge), check that

Wooden "caps" prevent water entering the end grain at the tops of the posts.

it is horizontal with a spirit-level, add a G-clamp to the central support post, and tighten all G-clamps. Now bore the holes to take the coach-bolts. The handrails do not need coach-bolts as heavy as the ones used to hold the supports (see the list of Materials on page 36), so the holes will be smaller. To prevent ugly holes being created as the drill breaks out on the far side of the wood slacken pressure on the drill just before it reaches the break-out point. Fix the rails to the posts at both ends of the bridge before fixing them to the centre posts.

FINISHING OFF

A nice touch is to add wooden "caps" to the top of the support posts – not just for decoration, but because the top of the posts expose the end grain to the atmosphere and will absorb rain. Wood caps, glued and screwed on to the post tops, prevent this.

A further final touch – before painting and other protective measures – is to screw panels of wood on to the ends of the bridge. This has to be left until last or it would be difficult to thread the nuts on the coach-bolts holding the handrail support posts to the bridge sides.

Now the bridge is ready for thorough coatings of a good wood preservative or paint.

# ADIRONDACK-STYLE CHAIR

THE ADIRONDACK MOUNTAINS OF NORTH-EAST NEW YORK STATE GIVE THEIR NAME TO A SPECIAL TYPE OF WOODEN ARMCHAIR. MADE ENTIRELY OF WOOD, THESE CHAIRS ARE DESIGNED IN SUCH A WAY AS TO BE SO COMFORTABLE THAT IT COMES AS A TERRIBLE WRENCH TO GET UP OFF ONE. BUT WHILE A REAL ADIRONDACK CHAIR TAKES SOME COMPLEX WOODWORKING TO BUILD, MY DESIGN NEEDS NO MORE THAN COMPETENCE IN DRIVING SCREWS INTO WOOD AND AN ABILITY TO USE A JIGSAW AND SPOKESHAVE. THE RESULT LOOKS GOOD, AND MAKES FOR COMFORTABLE AND RELAXED SITTING.

## TOOLS YOU WILL NEED

A TENON SAW
A JIGSAW
A PENCIL
A RULE OR MEASURE
A SCREWDRIVER
A DRILL
bit for screws
counterboring bit
A PLUG CUTTER
A SPOKESHAVE
A SMOOTHING PLANE
A CHISEL
WATERPROOF GLUE
GLASSPAPER
A PIECE OF CARDBOARD
for use as a template
A PIECE OF PLYWOOD
OR HARDBOARD
for reference
A BATTEN
for use as a "spacer"

**M**y version of the Adirondack chair is as close to the original as I could make it while at the same time eliminating any difficult shapes and involving none of the traditional jointing methods. The only real shaping to be done relates to the arms, which even then require only a jigsaw and a spokeshave. Otherwise this is an excellent project for all who are competent in gluing bits of wood together and putting screws in tightly – and most people can do that well enough.

I have deliberately designed the proportions of the chair to be generous. It is sufficiently deep to take a cushion at your back, while the front rails of the chair are far enough forward to support the whole of your thighs.

### STARTING OUT

**1** First, study the diagrams carefully. In particular, note that in order to keep the number of angles to a minimum I have constructed the chair essentially of two major parts: the squarish frame, comprising two flat sides joined horizontally by a couple of thin struts, and the seat,

which is also of two box-like sections (the seat itself and the back, both covered with slats), fastened at an angle between the sides of the frame. This angle is now the only angle to have to worry about – and if, as I recommend, you draw the side of the chair full size on a piece of plywood or hardboard, you will be able to position the struts of the frame against your drawing and mark off on to them exactly where the pieces making up the seat coincide.

### ASSEMBLING THE PARTS

**2** The frame comes first. The two sides are identical, except that one is the reverse of the other: there is a left side and a right side. Each side consists of three major planks: two verticals and a horizontal on the inside between them across the top. It is important to ensure that the two sides are equal in size, or the chair will simply not screw together. Be careful to drive in all the screws from the inside of the chair so that

**This Adirondack chair provides a comfortable place in which to sit and admire the garden.**

## MATERIALS

Wood:

planks/struts

battens

Zinc-plated Supascrews

Wood preservative

(see Cutting List)

when the whole chair is assembled they are not visible. To add stability to the chair legs, two horizontal struts are screwed onto the legs, as shown in the diagram, thus connecting the two sides. These struts prevent any possible flexing at the bottom of the legs, and add greatly to the overall strength of the chair.

**3** The seat is also made as a framework, the box that forms the basis for the back fitting inside the three members that form the basis for the seat: see the diagram. The struts of wood are simply butted together at the ends,

attached first with glue and then with zinc-plated screws. While the glue is still wet, check that both parts of the frame are square.

Once the frame is dry, fix on the nine vertical battens that form the back of the seat.

**4** The next task is to screw and glue the seat on to the flat sides. The screws for this must be of fairly large gauge: these screws take most the the weight of the chair's occupant and also hold the entire construction together.

Once the seat is fixed in position, it is time to attach the battens that the occupant actually sits

This view shows clearly the back frame of the chair onto which all the wooden chair slats are screwed.

## ADIRONDACK-STYLE CHAIR CUTTING LIST

**BACK**

**Verticals** 2 off 937 × 92 × 22 mm (36⅞ × 3⅝ × ⅞ in) timber

**Top and bottom struts** 2 off 565 × 92 × 22 mm (22¼ × 3⅝ × ⅞ in) timber

**Central cross-piece** 1 off 521 × 92 × 22 mm (20½ × 3⅝ × ⅞ in) timber

**Vertical battens** 9 off 937 × 47 × 22 mm (36⅞ × 1⅞ × ⅞ in) timber

**Top batten** 1 off 565 × 44 × 22 mm (22¼ × 1¾ × ⅞ in) timber

**SEAT**

**Side struts** 2 off 660 × 92 × 22 mm (26 × 3⅝ × ⅞ in) timber

**Front cross-piece** 1 off 610 × 114 × 22 mm (24 × 4½ × ⅞ in) timber

**Horizontal battens** 11 off 610 × 41 × 22 mm (24 × 1⅝ × ⅞ in) timber

1 off 610 × 32 × 22 mm (24 × 1¼ × ⅞ in) timber

**SIDE FRAMES**

**Verticals** 4 off 648 × 92 × 22 mm (25½ × 3⅝ × ⅞ in) timber

**Horizontals** 2 off 610 × 92 × 22 mm (24 × 3⅝ × ⅞ in) timber

**Lateral battens** 2 off 654 × 57 × 22 mm (25¾ × 2¼ × ⅞ in) timber

**Armrests** 2 off 724 × 117 × 22 mm (28½ × 4⅝ × ⅞ in) timber

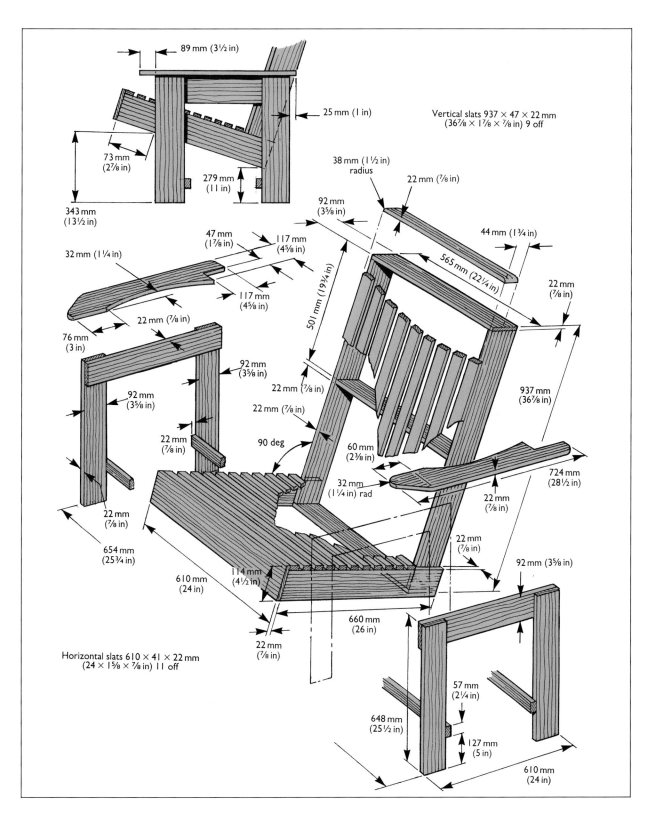

89 mm (3½ in)

25 mm (1 in)

73 mm (2⅞ in)

279 mm (11 in)

343 mm (13½ in)

Vertical slats 937 × 47 × 22 mm (36⅞ × 1⅞ × ⅞ in) 9 off

38 mm (1½ in) radius

22 mm (⅞ in)

92 mm (3⅝ in)

44 mm (1¾ in)

47 mm (1⅞ in)

117 mm (4⅝ in)

32 mm (1¼ in)

565 mm (22¼ in)

22 mm (⅞ in)

117 mm (4⅝ in)

501 mm (19¾ in)

22 mm (⅞ in)

76 mm (3 in)

92 mm (3⅝ in)

92 mm (3⅝ in)

22 mm (⅞ in)

22 mm (⅞ in)

90 deg

937 mm (36⅞ in)

60 mm (2⅜ in)

32 mm (1¼ in) rad

22 mm (⅞ in)

724 mm (28½ in)

22 mm (⅞ in)

22 mm (⅞ in)

92 mm (3⅝ in)

654 mm (25¾ in)

610 mm (24 in)

114 mm (4½ in)

660 mm (26 in)

22 mm (⅞ in)

Horizontal slats 610 × 41 × 22 mm (24 × 1⅝ × ⅞ in) 11 off

57 mm (2¼ in)

648 mm (25½ in)

127 mm (5 in)

610 mm (24 in)

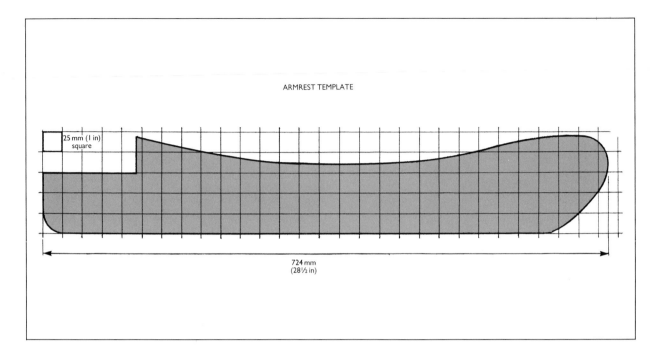

ARMREST TEMPLATE

25 mm (1 in)
square

724 mm
(28½ in)

on. First fix on the batten at the front of the chair, against the frame member. To avoid measuring over and over the space between subsequent battens, make a "spacer" from spare batten of exactly the width of the interval between seat battens, and use it in turn to position the remaining ten battens.

At the front of the chair, on the frame member, a wider batten can be screwed. The edges of this batten and all the others on the seat should be chamfered off with a smoothing plane.

Similarly, a length of batten can be fitted along the top of the back of the seat, and also rounded at the edges. This batten gives a finished look to the seat.

**5** Finally, the arms require some time to be spent on their shaping. The best way to achieve the desired shape is to copy it in pencil on a large sheet of cardboard, using the squared grid lines provided here as reference. Cut the shape out of the cardboard, and use it as a template to transfer the shape to a plank of wood.

There are several types of saw capable of cutting out the arm's shape, but the quickest is surely the electric jigsaw (which is ideal for this sort of work). When the arm has been cut out, remove all the rough saw cuts with a spokeshave.

The last piece of shaping necessary is to cut the angle where the arm meets the sloping seat back. The angle in the cross-section of the arm must be at the same slope. Use a tenon saw and a sharp chisel – and be patient until it fits well.

Once in position, the arm is fixed to the frame by glue and screws. To hide the screws I strongly recommend counterboring each screw hole to some depth, and cutting a wood plug to fit in the top over the screw head. Glue in the plug: any excess wood can be shaved off when the glue is dry.

FINISHING OFF

Last of all, work all over the entire construction with fine glasspaper. Make utterly certain that there are no wood splinters or snags to spoil clothes.

Coat the chair with a good wood preservative.

# LETTERBOX

IF YOU HAVE A LONG DRIVEWAY UP TO YOUR HOUSE,
OR A DOG THAT EATS YOUR LETTERS AS THEY COME
THROUGH THE DOOR, THEN IT IS A GOOD IDEA TO
MAKE AN EXTERIOR LETTERBOX.

**T**his box can be freestanding, on a post with legs (as illustrated), or fixed to a fence or gateway. A freestanding box will have to be secured to the ground with wooden pegs or elongated metal staples through the legs at the base, or with the post solidly anchored in the grasp of a commercially available steel socket with a spiked tip.

My design is intended to be both practical (accepting all the most common sizes and shapes of envelopes) and weatherproof; the tongued-and-grooved boarding I recommend is also attractive. I have deliberately used the boarding vertically rather than horizontally so that water drains off readily, and to assist in drainage even further the base is chamfered around the top edge. Wood – even untreated wood – will last for many years provided that water is not trapped in cracks and crevices.

## STARTING OUT

**1** First, study the drawing. You are going to begin by making the sides, so note that left and right sides are different. Bear this in mind, and double-check when arranging your boards. Cut all the boards to length. Carefully fix the side boards together, aligning them at the bottom edge. Then pencil in the slope across the top.

**Your postman will be delighted to find one of these at your entrance – thus saving his legs.**

## TOOLS YOU WILL NEED

A SAW
A COPING SAW *or*
A JIGSAW
A PENCIL
A RULE OR MEASURE
A SCREWDRIVER
A DRILL
bit for screws
counterbore bit
flat bit
A PLUG CUTTER
A SMOOTHING PLANE
WATERPROOF GLUE
GLASSPAPER

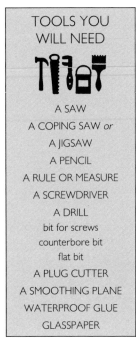

## MATERIALS

Wood:
- tongued-and- grooved boards
- battens
- post (and legs)
- dowel rods

Zinc-plated Supascrews
Brass recessed hinge(s) and screws
Nylon cord
Wood preservative
(Metal eyes or loops)
(Padlock)
(see Cutting List)

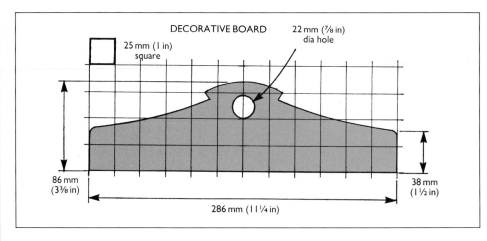

DECORATIVE BOARD
22 mm (⅞ in)
dia hole
25 mm (1 in)
square
86 mm
(3⅜ in)
38 mm
(1½ in)
286 mm (11¼ in)

The next operation is to glue and screw small battens of wood along the top and bottom inside edges: the top edge is represented by your sloping pencil line. Check with the diagram to make sure you have arranged the battens correctly, and screw from the batten (inner) side so that screw heads do not appear on the exterior of the letterbox. Once the glue and screws are in place, the waste wood at the top – the angle left by the slope – can be sawn off to leave a clean sloping edge.

### ASSEMBLING THE PARTS

**2** The back and front pieces of the box are made in identical fashion: the only difference between them is their vertical height. Again battens are glued to top and bottom inside edges.

Once all four sides have been made, the letterbox is glued and screwed together. To conceal the screws, counterbore the holes before driving in the screws and then fill in the counterbore holes with wooden plugs drilled out of the appropriate board using a plug cutter. The plugs should be glued over the tops of the screws. When the four sides are complete and together – but before the glue has cured (set) – check that the whole box is square.

Once the four sides are solid, there is some planing to do on them. The flat top of the front piece should be planed down to the angle of the

## LETTERBOX CUTTING LIST

**Post** 1 off 1105 × 67 × 67 mm (43½ × 2⅝ × 2⅝ in) timber

**Feet** 4 off 406 × 70 × 22 mm (16 × 2¾ × ⅞ in) timber

**Capping plate** 1 off 95 × 83 × 16 mm (3¾ × 3¼ × ⅝ in) timber

**Support bracket** 1 off 222 × 124 × 22 mm (8¾ × 4⅞ × ⅞ in) timber

**Box sides and base** make from 4875 × 89 × 16 mm (192 × 3½ × ⅝ in) V-machined tongued-and-grooved boarding

**Box battens** make from 1020 × 22 × 16 mm (40 × ⅞ × ⅝ in) timber

**Lid** make from 1700 × 89 × 16 mm (67 × 3½ × ⅝ in) V-machined tongued-and-grooved boarding

**Lid battens** 2 off 286 × 22 × 16 mm (11¼ × ⅞ × ⅝ in) timber
1 off 305 × 22 × 16 mm (12 × ⅞ × ⅝ in) timber

**Headboard** 1 off 286 × 83 × 16 mm (11¼ × 3¼ × ⅝ in) timber

**Dowel** 1 off 9 mm diam. × 67 mm length (⅜ in diam. × 2⅝ in length) dowel rod

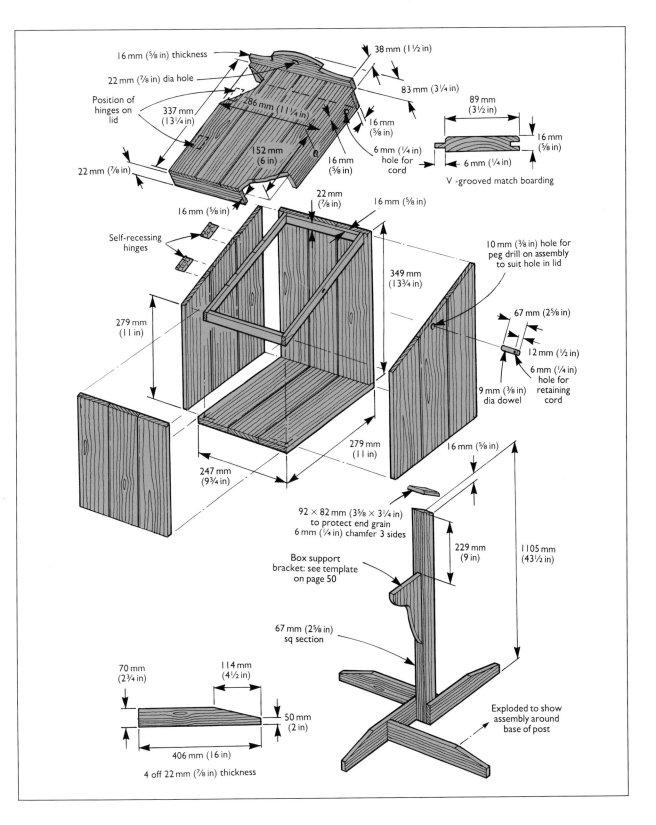

16 mm (⅝ in) thickness

22 mm (⅞ in) dia hole

Position of hinges on lid

337 mm (13¼ in)

286 mm (11¼ in)

152 mm (6 in)

22 mm (⅞ in)

16 mm (⅝ in)

38 mm (1½ in)

83 mm (3¼ in)

16 mm (⅝ in)

6 mm (¼ in) hole for cord

89 mm (3½ in)

16 mm (⅝ in)

6 mm (¼ in)

V-grooved match boarding

Self-recessing hinges

16 mm (⅝ in)

22 mm (⅞ in)

16 mm (⅝ in)

10 mm (⅜ in) hole for peg drill on assembly to suit hole in lid

349 mm (13¾ in)

67 mm (2⅝ in)

12 mm (½ in)

6 mm (¼ in) hole for retaining cord

9 mm (⅜ in) dia dowel

279 mm (11 in)

247 mm (9¾ in)

279 mm (11 in)

16 mm (⅝ in)

92 × 82 mm (3⅝ × 3¼ in) to protect end grain
6 mm (¼ in) chamfer 3 sides

Box support bracket: see template on page 50

67 mm (2⅝ in) sq section

229 mm (9 in)

1105 mm (43½ in)

70 mm (2¾ in)

114 mm (4½ in)

50 mm (2 in)

406 mm (16 in)

4 off 22 mm (⅞ in) thickness

Exploded to show assembly around base of post

49

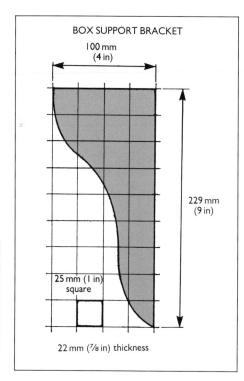

BOX SUPPORT BRACKET

100 mm
(4 in)

229 mm
(9 in)

25 mm (1 in)
square

22 mm (⁷/₈ in) thickness

### USEFUL TIP

The advantage of side-hinging the lid ensures that you can mount the letterbox on a wall, while still allowing the lid to open completely.

sloping sides that adjoin it, or the lid will not shut properly. Use a sharp plane to trim off the angle. Then use the plane gently to trim quite flat the bottom and sloping edges. (The bottom edge has to be flat in order to take the base.)

**3** The base is made from tongued-and-grooved floorboarding, the top and bottom edges of which are square (with no decorative groove). Square off the other edges by trimming the tongue off one and the groove off the other, using a plane. Trim the whole base a little smaller than the sides. Use the plane also to create a slight chamfer on the top edge: this will help to shed water that runs down the side of the box. Glue and screw the base to the sides.

**4** Like the sides, the lid is made of tongued-and-grooved V-machined boards. The lid made, battens are glued and screwed on the top, the bottom, and the front side of the box. There is no batten on the hinged side, or the lid would be prevented from opening wide. As before, drive the screws in from the interior side of the box. The small, decorative headboard at the top must be shaped using a coping saw or a jigsaw, and is then glued and screwed on to the top of the letterbox.

**5** The best type of hinge to fit is the recessed variety, made of brass. The great advantage of this readily available hinge is that there is no need to cut away "slots" of wood to take the leaves of the hinge. To fit, position the hinges on the box, position the lid on the hinges, and mark everything with a pencil – hinge outlines and screw holes. Remove the lid, screw each hinge on to the box and, after drilling small pilot holes, fix the lid to the hinges. That is all there is to it. But do make sure you use brass screws with the brass hinges.

**6** When the lid is in place, carefully drill a hole through the side batten using a large flat bit just a fraction larger than the diameter of the dowel rod. Care is needed, for it is important that this hole looks neat: a thin piece of waste wood placed between the side of the box and the batten before you drill may be an added

The lid is hinged from the side, allowing the box to be fitted against a gate or wall.

security against an ugly hole.

**7** Cut a length of dowel rod to size (see diagram), and chamfer the ends with glasspaper. Drill a hole through one end of the dowel rod, and another hole of the same dimensions through the side batten at the top. Thread a length of nylon cord through both holes and fasten with a knot at both ends, so that the dowel rod remains suspended by the cord from the batten when it is not securing the lid.

**8** The post is now cut to length. The top of the post should be cut at an angle to help water to run off. The feet of the post are simply cut to shape, and glued and screwed to the base of the post: glue and screw each leg to one side, turn the post around, and repeat the process with another leg.

## FIXING THE LETTERBOX TO THE POST

**9** To screw the letterbox to the post, the best method is to drill holes from the outside at an upward angle. The screws can then be fitted from inside the box, and driven downward into the post – the angle of the holes greatly increases the ease with which the screws can be driven in from the inside.

A wooden bracket fitted to the underneath of the box is not strictly necessary, but it does improve the look of the whole construction (and prevents the box from appearing to be simply transfixed on its post). The bracket is glued on to the post and further secured by a screw that passes though from the inside base of the box.

A short length of tongued-and-grooved board is glued on to the top of the post to prevent rainwater from seeping into the top of the post.

Finally, drill a couple of small holes in the bottom of the box, just in case water should ever get in, and give the entire construction a coating of a good wood preservative.

## FINISHING OFF

That the lid is held shut by a dowel rod (in the approved country fashion) will be sufficient for most people, but some may require a bit more security. In that case, two metal loops or eyes that overlap can easily be fixed to lid and front, to be fastened there with a padlock.

Timber is amazingly resilient to water, especially if well treated with a preservative. However, it is advisable to make sure that the tops of the posts, where end grain is exposed to rain, are covered with a wooden cap. Here, a length of tongued-and-grooved board has been used.

# FOR THE GARDENER

IT'S SO EASY TO ENHANCE YOUR GARDEN WITH A FEW

WELL-PLACED FEATURES SUCH AS PLANT TROUGHS,

WINDOW BOXES OR DECORATIVE WHEELBARROWS.

IN THIS SECTION, THESE PROJECTS, TOGETHER WITH SOME

A LITTLE MORE ADVENTUROUS, WILL ENSURE THAT

THERE IS ALWAYS SOMEWHERE TO GROW, TRAIL OR

DISPLAY BEAUTIFUL PLANTS.

# TRELLIS AND LADDER

IF YOU ARE ONE OF THOSE PEOPLE WHO ARE APPREHENSIVE ABOUT WOODWORKING, OR FIND IT FRUSTRATINGLY DIFFICULT, YOU MAY WELL BE SITTING COMFORTABLY SOMEWHERE, THUMBING THROUGH THIS BOOK AND MUTTERING TO YOURSELF: "ALL THIS IS JUST TOO COMPLICATED FOR ME. WHEN IS THERE GOING TO BE SOMETHING I CAN MAKE?" WELL, THIS IS IT.

S tudy the pictures, look closely at the construction diagrams – and you are more than half-way there already. Trellis and ladder construction is really no more than fixing two bits of wood together many times over, and most people can do that well enough. A little care – and a good glue to ensure that what you fix stays fixed – and the result should be fine.

## THE TRELLIS
The trellis consists of a framework of three main pieces of wood – a central vertical post and two horizontal cross-pieces – and a quantity of battens fixed across them. In the method I describe below I have suggested that the horizontal struts of the framework have square sections cut out of them to fit snugly around the vertical post, so giving the structure some added rigidity (and overall strength). If you are not confident of doing this, it isn't entirely necessary – but the structure will undoubtedly be better for it if you can manage it.

1 First study the diagram, and ensure that your wood is of the right type and lengths. Now make up your mind if you are going to cut the square sections out of the horizontal struts.

2 If you are going to use these "half-halving joints", make a start by marking on to the centre of each horizontal strut the width of the vertical post, using a pencil and, afterwards, a carpenter's knife (or artist's knife or scalpel). With a rule and a pencil, mark the depth of the section to be cut out. Use a tenon saw to cut vertically into each strut down the two sides of the depth just marked, and chisel out the waste wood between the cuts. (If this is the first time you have attempted chiselling like this, you may be surprised at how easily the wood chips out.) Do not chisel it all out from just the one side: turn the wood around and chisel some from the other side. To end, make a fine cut along the bottom of the joint.

The joint should fit so that the horizontal strut and vertical post are hand-tight together, and perpendicular to each other.

If it is not tight, then a generous quantity of glue and two large screws or nails should certainly make sure of it!

The Trellis is a very simple but effective piece of garden furniture. Shown here attached to the Barbecue Shelter, it takes off the "squareness" of the design. Trellis can easily be attached to any garden or house wall.

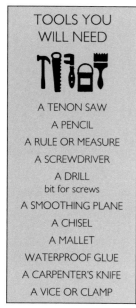

## TOOLS YOU WILL NEED

A TENON SAW
A PENCIL
A RULE OR MEASURE
A SCREWDRIVER
A DRILL
bit for screws
A SMOOTHING PLANE
A CHISEL
A MALLET
WATERPROOF GLUE
A CARPENTER'S KNIFE
A VICE OR CLAMP

## MATERIALS

Wood:
  trellis framework struts
  battens
  rung struts/end rails
  ladder lengths
Zinc-plated Supascrews
Wood preservative
(Nails)
(see Cutting List)

And if all this cutting and chiselling is too much to contemplate in the first place, then glue and screws or nails in the same quantities will effect the whole job perfectly well without.

**3** Once the horizontal struts have been securely attached to the vertical post, the time has come to fix on the battens. Using screws to attach them is better than using nails – nails would do, but might split the battens. Drill small pilot holes before driving in the screws. And use screws again where battens intersect: this adds further rigidity.

In this way, a trellis can be made to any size or even shape: it really is quite straightforward.

### THE LADDER

The ornamental ladder is almost as easy to construct. The idea is that it adds a decorative touch along the top of two trellises made in the fashion just described.

**1** Make a start with the rungs. The rungs have to be shaped: mark out in pencil and then with a

A half-halving joint is used when constructing the Trellis. The tools used for this are the tenon saw, chisel and mallet.

saw cut a taper at each end of each rung. Remove the rough saw marks using a plane, and, to save time, plane two at a time together in the vice. When planing, take care not to plane farther than the original pencil markings. The

The ladder is screwed to the Trellis at one end and to the Barbecue Shelter at the other (see page 12).

## TRELLIS AND LADDER CUTTING LIST

**TRELLIS**

**Main vertical** 1 off 2286 × 44 × 44 mm (90 × 1¾ × 1¾ in) timber

**Top cross-piece** 1 off 791 × 44 × 44 mm (31⅛ × 1¾ × 1¾ in) timber

**Bottom cross-piece** 1 off 400 × 44 × 44 mm (15¾ × 1¾ × 1¾ in) timber

**Vertical battens** 5 off 2070 × 22 × 19 mm (81½ × ⅞ × ¾ in) timber

**Horizontal battens** make from 6100 × 22 × 19 mm (240 × ⅞ × ¾ in) timber

**LADDER**

**Ladder lengths** 2 off 1168 × 44 × 44 mm (46 × 1¾ × 1¾ in) timber

**Laterals** 2 off 635 × 44 × 44 mm (25 × 1¾ × 1¾ in) timber

**Rungs (tie-bars)** 4 off 762 × 70 × 22 mm (30 × 2¾ × ⅞ in) timber

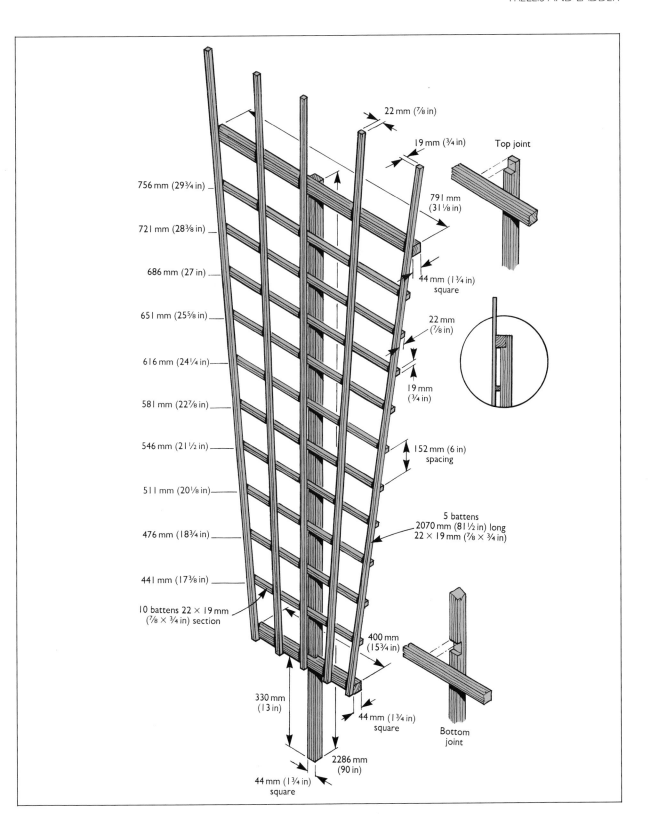

22 mm (⅞ in)

19 mm (¾ in)

Top joint

756 mm (29¾ in)

721 mm (28⅜ in)

686 mm (27 in)

791 mm (31⅛ in)

651 mm (25⅝ in)

44 mm (1¾ in) square

616 mm (24¼ in)

22 mm (⅞ in)

581 mm (22⅞ in)

19 mm (¾ in)

546 mm (21½ in)

152 mm (6 in) spacing

511 mm (20⅛ in)

5 battens
2070 mm (81½ in) long
22 × 19 mm (⅞ × ¾ in)

476 mm (18¾ in)

441 mm (17⅜ in)

10 battens 22 × 19 mm (⅞ × ¾ in) section

400 mm (15¾ in)

330 mm (13 in)

44 mm (1¾ in) square

Bottom joint

2286 mm (90 in)

44 mm (1¾ in) square

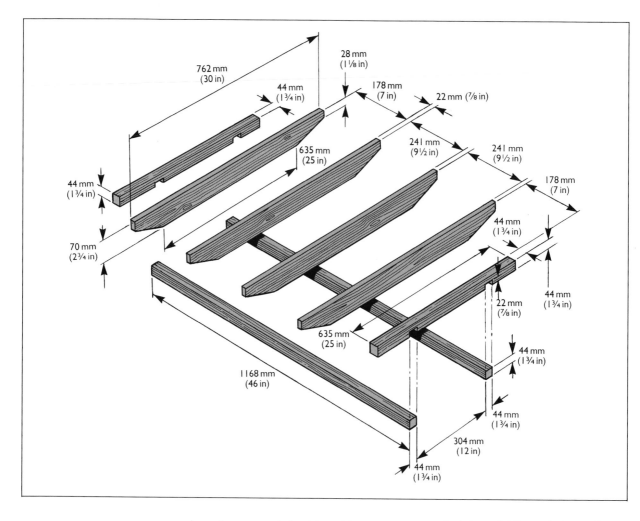

number of rungs, and the interval between them (which should be constant), is up to you.

**2** The rungs have then to be attached to the two ladder lengths. Again screws are best although nails would do. Drill pilot holes for the screws before driving them in.

To add rigidity to the ladder, an unshaped strut or rail should be attached firmly at each end, between the lengths and parallel with the rungs, using the same "half-halving joint" used in the trellis framework. A section equal to the depth of the ladder length is cut out from each end of each rail. The end rails are then glued and screwed in position.

It is with these end rails that the ladder is attached to the two trellises, although the rails

are particularly useful if you decide to fix one end of your ladder to a wall instead. On the other hand, how you finish off the ladder ends may depend where in the garden – or even around the house – you intend to position the whole trellis and ladder construction.

**3** Use screws to fix the ladder to the top of the trellis. Apart from anything else, it is easier than standing on a stepladder and trying to bang in nails.

FINISHING OFF

It is essential that the wood of the entire construction – trellis and ladder – is treated with a good wood preservative.

# PERGOLA

THIS IS ONE OF THE SIMPLEST PIECES OF GARDEN FURNITURE TO MAKE – AND IT IS EASY TO ADAPT MY DESIGN TO MAKE SOMETHING SIMILAR THAT IS MORE SUITED TO YOUR PARTICULAR GARDEN FOR ONE REASON OR ANOTHER.

This pergola can even be made using nails instead of screws – although I cannot really recommend doing so, for nails may pull out or may split wood when being hammered in, whereas screws never work loose. Nails also have to be hammered home on a firm surface (such as a garage floor), whereas screws can be used to bring two pieces of wood together without any such backing. Personally, for my garden projects I always use zinc-plated Supascrews.

## STARTING OUT

**1** First, study the diagram. Consider in particular how you intend to fix your structure into the ground. I like to use purpose-made steel sockets with spiked tips, commercially available in all the standard post sizes, which can be driven into the ground fairly easily and which allow good drainage so that the wood placed in them is prevented from rotting. They are sold under different trade names in different countries, but represent probably the simplest and best method of fixing posts in the ground. The principal alternative is to bury the feet of the posts themselves in prepared ground – never fix wooden posts into the ground with concrete – in which case a minimum depth of 30 cm (12 in) should be observed.

**2** Make a start by constructing the sides. Cut the vertical and horizontal struts to length. Then attach two of the horizontal struts to two vertical struts: one at the top of the vertical struts, the other near the bottom – but leaving enough of the vertical struts projecting downwards either to fit into the steel sockets or to be buried in the ground themselves. Repeat the process with the struts that make up the other side.

Check both side frames for squareness by laying them flat on the ground and, with a long rod, making sure that measurements from corner to opposite diagonal corner are all equal and identical.

**3** To make the trellis you will need a quantity of battens. I recommend purchasing one or more packs of what are called tile battens, generally available at woodyards or builder's merchants (and used mostly to fix tiles on roofs). They are made in various sizes, some of which are ideal for constructing trellises – so much easier than trying to cut your own battens from planks. It is possible to buy tile battens already treated with wood preservative, but there is no need for you to do so if you are going to treat the whole construction with preservative later – as I suggest in due course.

## ASSEMBLING THE PARTS

Having obtained your battens, first cut to length those that are to be attached vertically. The best method for this is to cut as many as possible all at

the same time, clamping them together before sawing. Then fix the battens at top and bottom to both pairs of horizontals of the frame, using screws or nails.

**4** Next, cut to length the battens that are to be the horizontal struts of the trellis. Again cut as many as possible all at once, clamped together. The battens are threaded in under the vertical battens before being fixed at the ends, using screws or nails.

To add some rigidity – and therefore strength – to the side panels, it is helpful at this point to screw or nail some of the vertical and horizontal battens together where they intersect. You do not need to screw or nail every intersection: a dozen or so, well spaced out, should do.

Your two side panels are now complete.

**5** To connect the side panels to each other, most structures of this type use a fairly wide

*Above:* Timbers and battens screwed into place at the top of one of the four vertical posts.
*Right:* This handsome wooden structure is built mainly from very inexpensive roofing batten.

headboard – and my design is no exception. Choose your headboard and use a saw to taper the ends.

**6** It can be quite tricky actually to attach the headboard to the two side panels. You may have to call upon the aid of a second pair of hands at this stage, or, failing that, of a nearby wall or large box, against which to prop up one panel while you work on the other and the headboard.

Once you have organized the positioning of the structure, fix the headboard to the end of each side panel. Even though elsewhere in this construction the use of screws or nails has been optional, for this particular operation it is advisable to use screws.

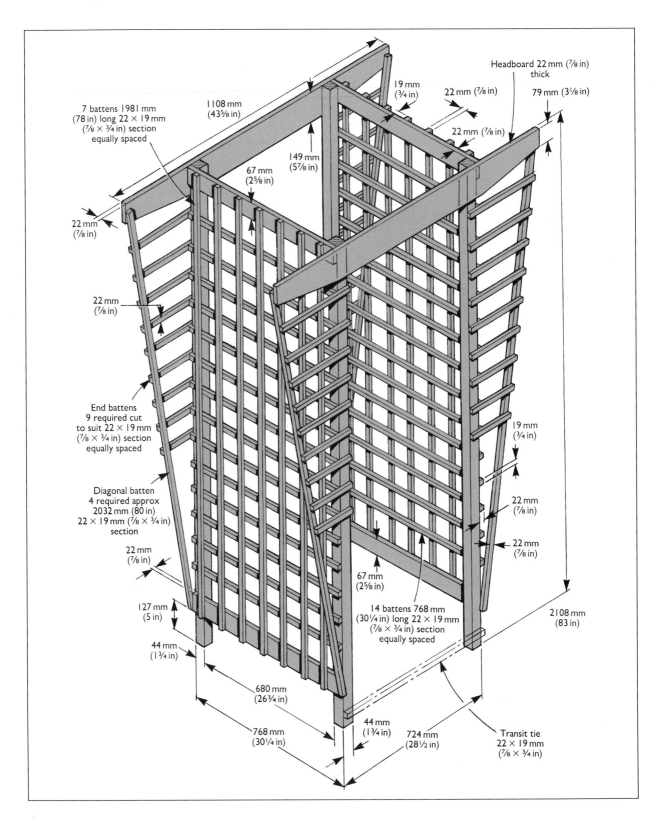

7 battens 1981 mm (78 in) long 22 × 19 mm (⁷⁄₈ × ³⁄₄ in) section equally spaced

1108 mm (43⁵⁄₈ in)

19 mm (³⁄₄ in)

22 mm (⁷⁄₈ in)

Headboard 22 mm (⁷⁄₈ in) thick

79 mm (3¹⁄₈ in)

22 mm (⁷⁄₈ in)

149 mm (5⁷⁄₈ in)

67 mm (2⁵⁄₈ in)

22 mm (⁷⁄₈ in)

22 mm (⁷⁄₈ in)

End battens 9 required cut to suit 22 × 19 mm (⁷⁄₈ × ³⁄₄ in) section equally spaced

19 mm (³⁄₄ in)

Diagonal batten 4 required approx 2032 mm (80 in) 22 × 19 mm (⁷⁄₈ × ³⁄₄ in) section

22 mm (⁷⁄₈ in)

22 mm (⁷⁄₈ in)

22 mm (⁷⁄₈ in)

67 mm (2⁵⁄₈ in)

2108 mm (83 in)

127 mm (5 in)

44 mm (1³⁄₄ in)

680 mm (26³⁄₄ in)

14 battens 768 mm (30¹⁄₄ in) long 22 × 19 mm (⁷⁄₈ × ³⁄₄ in) section equally spaced

768 mm (30¹⁄₄ in)

44 mm (1³⁄₄ in)

724 mm (28¹⁄₂ in)

Transit tie 22 × 19 mm (⁷⁄₈ × ³⁄₄ in)

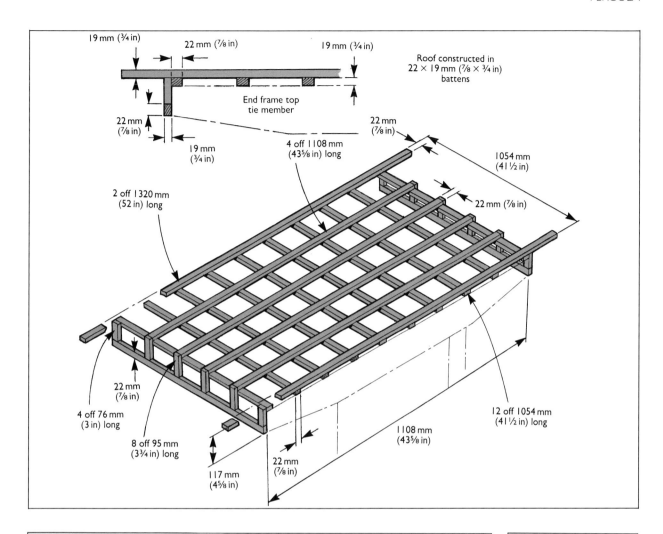

19 mm (¾ in)
22 mm (⅞ in)
19 mm (¾ in)
Roof constructed in
22 × 19 mm (⅞ × ¾ in)
battens

End frame top
tie member

22 mm
(⅞ in)

19 mm
(¾ in)

4 off 1108 mm
(43⅝ in) long

22 mm
(⅞ in)

1054 mm
(41½ in)

22 mm (⅞ in)

2 off 1320 mm
(52 in) long

22 mm
(⅞ in)

4 off 76 mm
(3 in) long

8 off 95 mm
(3¾ in) long

12 off 1054 mm
(41½ in) long

1108 mm
(43⅝ in)

117 mm
(4⅝ in)

22 mm
(⅞ in)

## PERGOLA CUTTING LIST

### SIDE FRAMES

**Vertical struts** 4 off 2108 × 44 × 44 mm (83 ×
1¾ × 1¾ in) timber

**Horizontal struts** 4 off 768 × 67 × 22 mm
(30¼ × 2⅝ × ⅞ in) timber

**Vertical battens** 14 off 1981 × 22 × 19 mm
(78 × ⅞ × ¾ in) timber

**Horizontal battens** 28 off 768 × 22 × 19 mm
(30¼ × ⅞ × ¾ in) timber

### LINKING SUPPORTS

**Headboard** 2 off 1108 × 149 × 22 mm (43⅝ ×
5⅞ × ⅞ in) timber

**Transit tie** 2 off 724 × 22 × 19 mm (28½ × ⅞
× ¾ in) timber

**Sloping battens** 4 off 2032 × 22 × 19 mm (80
× ⅞ × ¾ in) timber

**Subbrace battens** make from 6600 × 22 ×
19 mm (260 × ⅞ × ¾ in) timber

### ROOF (AS ILLUSTRATED)

**Outer cross-battens** 2 off 1320 × 22 × 19 mm
(52 × ⅞ × ¾ in) timber

**Intermediate cross-battens** 4 off 1108 × 22
× 19 mm (43⅝ × ⅞ × ¾ in) timber

**Longitudinal battens** 12 off 1054 × 22 ×
19 mm (41½ × ⅞ × ¾ in) timber

**Outer vertical battens** 4 off 76 × 22 × 19 mm
(3 × ⅞ × ¾ in) timber

**Intermediate vertical battens** 8 off 95 × 22
× 19 mm (3¾ × ⅞ × ¾ in) timber

## MATERIALS

Wood:
  posts and struts
  board (for headboard)
  tile battens
Zinc-plated Supascrews,
  *and/or*
Nails
Wood preservative
(Post-fixing steel sockets
  with spiked tips)
(see Cutting List)

When the initial screws have been driven in, check that at the bottom the ends of the side panels are exactly as far apart as they are at the top by the headboard.

**7** One of the great weaknesses of this sort of structure is that until it is solidly placed in the ground, the bottom edges of the side panels are all too free to move, even when the headboard has been attached at the top of one end. For this reason I have included in my design a method of bracing the side panels against the headboard.

A length of batten is screwed on to each of the two outside edges of the headboard, connecting with the foot of the side panel end post on its own side, to which it is also screwed. The batten, fixed at an angle in this way, is not only useful in bracing the structure but is itself an attractive feature of the trellis – and can be made even more attractive. Short lengths of batten are then glued and screwed to attach the batten to the side panel end posts at intervals all the way down. These too are both decorative and functional, giving additional rigidity to the overall construction.

Complete the batten and its attendant subbraces on one side before turning the entire structure over and repeating the process on the other side.

**8** Only now is it time to fix battens across the top, creating a roof between the side panels. Ordinary parallel struts are perfectly acceptable, but you may wish to employ a more adventurous latticework design of your own devising.

### FINISHING OFF

Until the structure is fixed into the ground in its permanent site – and especially while it is being moved around – it is a good idea to screw a couple of offcut battens across the bottoms of the side panels to maintain rigidity and reduce the likelihood of damage.

It is essential that the entire construction is treated with a good wood preservative.

**Vertical posts are held together at the top by two planks of wood.**

# GARDEN GATE AND FENCE

A GARDEN GATE DOES NOT HAVE TO MARK THE ENTRANCE TO YOUR GARDEN FROM THE STREET. WITH A FENCE IT CAN PROVIDE SOME PLEASANTLY SECLUDED AREAS OF A GARDEN WITHIN A GARDEN. A FENCE CAN SIMILARLY BE USED FOR MORE THAN MERELY KEEPING ANIMALS OR PEOPLE OUT (OR IN), AND MAY BE A DECORATIVE FEATURE IN ITS OWN RIGHT.

**N**ot too long ago, the village carpenter used to make gates for the farmers and country cottagers of the local countryside. The gates he made for them were simple and robust, stylish even without the decoration he might have added to gates meant for the grander homes of the squires and other gentry. My design is based on this tradition, intended to be as simple and yet as stylish, yet requiring only screws and glue (rather than the traditional mortice-and-tenon joints) to put it together.

Before you begin construction, however, it may well be worth your while first to take a look at one or more books on overall garden design: my text and diagrams are meant only to give you practical guidance on how to make the gate and the fence — not on how your garden will look afterwards. Variants may be more or less suitable for your needs. A lower fence, for example, painted white could look especially attractive in a smaller or sloping garden.

## THE GATE

If the idea of building a garden gate fills you with trepidation, you are not alone. This was my first gate too. But as you will see, it turned out to be perfectly straightforward.

**1** First study the diagrams, and check that the wood you have is suitable in every respect.

Make a start by selecting three struts as the horizontal rails of the gate. If possible, the struts should be free of knots, and flat (without twists). Determine on the width of the gate, and cut the struts to that length: an average gate width might be the same as the average width of a door – say 75 cm (2 ft 6 in) – but remember that it may be necessary to be able to wheel a wheelbarrow through the garden gate: make sure it is wide enough for it.

**2** Now select the vertical struts (pales). Again, if possible, these should be knot-free and flat. Clamp them all together, and pencil in on them the position of the three horizontal rails. (The best method is actually to lay the horizontal rails across the vertical struts, and mark directly off their width. Do not attach the horizontals to the verticals yet.)

**3** With a pencil mark up all the corners of the tops of the vertical struts, and with a saw, saw them off. Using a smoothing plane, then smooth off the rough saw marks. In fact, you could also run the plane down all the sides of the struts to remove the sharp edges: this will soften the lines of the finished gate and enhance its appeal.

**4** The vertical rails are now glued and screwed on to the three horizontal struts. Before driving the screws in, drill pilot holes for the screws and countersink the holes (using a countersink bit):

this reduces the possibility of the screw heads' shearing off or the wood's splitting, and ensures that the screw heads bed down properly. Also before driving the screws in, coat adjoining surfaces with waterproof glue. Then drive in the twin-threaded zinc-plated screws.

**5** Now all that remains on the gate is to make the two diagonal braces that prevent the gate from sagging. To ensure a tight fit, put a length of wood up against the horizontal struts of the gate, and mark off on it with a pencil the angles it is necessary to cut: marking directly against the gate is guaranteed to produce accurate results. The second brace is marked off and cut in exactly the same way.

Glue and screw the braces in position using the method outlined above (see Step 4). The gate is then complete.

## THE GATEPOSTS AND SURROUNDS
Having gone to such trouble to make the gate, it would be a pity not to try to do something special with the gateposts, from one of which the gate will hang on hinges, and on to the other of which it may latch. My design has a simple wooden trellis between the gateposts, across the top.

**1** Study the diagram to make clear in your mind what has to be done. Select two posts – perhaps the standard 50 mm × 50 mm (2 in × 2 in). Set them up apart from each other by 6 mm ($\frac{1}{4}$ in) *more* than the width of the gate, and hold them

*Right:* By the addition of a trellis top a simple gate can add greatly to any field or garden setting.
*Below:* This detail shows the top of one of the vertical gate posts and how the Trellis is fixed.

## MATERIALS

Wood:

 struts

 posts

 battens

Zinc-plated Supascrews

Twin-threaded Supascrews

Black, japanned T-bar hinges

 and screws

Gate-latch

Post-fixing steel sockets

 with sharp tip

Wood preservative

(Varnish/paint)

(see Cutting List)

in that position by temporarily attaching a batten between them at the bottom. Screw the batten in at both ends: it can be removed when the time comes for sinking the posts into the ground.

**2** All this is so as to complete the fairly simple trellis-work across the top. It comprises a framework made up of two main ties fixed one each side of the gateposts, forming the major linking component of the arch, and up to nine cross-pieces hanging underneath, all supported by two lighter longitudinal members (secondary ties) that run along the outside of the top. The cross-pieces are screwed in position from the underside, and are of sufficient width to require the screws to be counterbored. Moreover, once the trellis has been fixed together it is worth filling the counterbore holes with wood plugs (for which you will need a plug cutter).

This detail shows the diagonal bracing of the gate, its T-bar black hinge and the simple latch to keep the gate closed.

## GARDEN GATE AND FENCE CUTTING LIST

**THE FENCE: 6-PALE SECTION**

**Vertical struts (pales)** 6 off 864 × 73 × 22 mm (34 × 2⅞ × ⅞ in) timber

**Horizontal rails** 2 off 978 × 73 × 22 mm (38½ × 2⅞ × ⅞ in) timber

**THE FENCE: 9-PALE SECTION**

**Vertical struts (pales)** 9 off 864 × 73 × 22 mm (34 × 2⅞ × ⅞ in) timber

**Horizontal rails** 2 off 1257 × 73 × 22mm (49½ × 2⅞ × ⅞ in) timber

**THE GATE**

**Vertical struts (pales)** 7 off 1016 × 67 × 22 mm (40 × 2⅝ × ⅞ in) timber

**Horizontal rails** 3 off 759 × 67 × 22 mm (29⅞ × 2⅝ × ⅞ in) timber

**Diagonal braces** 2 off 829 × 67 × 22 mm (32⅝ × 2⅝ × ⅞ in) timber

**GATEPOSTS AND TRELLIS**

**Gateposts** 2 off 2337 × 48 × 48 mm (92 × 1⅞ × 1⅞ in) timber

**Main ties** 2 off 1321 × 48 × 48 mm (52 × 1⅞ × 1⅞ in) timber

**Cross-pieces** 9 off 622 × 67 × 22 mm (24½ × 2⅝ × ⅞ in) timber

**Secondary ties** 2 off 1321 × 22 × 16 mm (52 × ⅞ × ⅝ in) timber

**Temporary batten** 1 off 1219 × 44 × 22 mm (48 × 1¾ × ⅞ in) timber

**3** When the gateposts have been completed, it is time to put the hinges on the gate and attach the gate to the posts.

The hinges I recommend are the T-bar black japanned type, which are relatively easy to fit, using the accompanying round-headed black japanned screws. The thick black paint on hinges and screws mean that they will not rust for many years – although there is a drawback. You will find that once you have fitted all the screws, no matter how careful you may have been, the screwdriver will have – perhaps ever so slightly

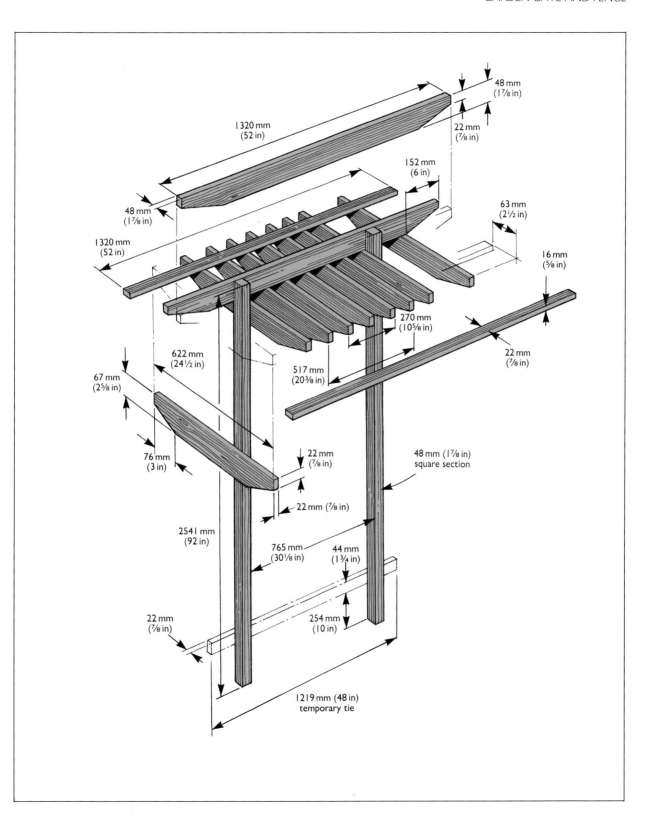

1320 mm
(52 in)

48 mm
(1⅞ in)

22 mm
(⅞ in)

152 mm
(6 in)

63 mm
(2½ in)

48 mm
(1⅞ in)

1320 mm
(52 in)

16 mm
(⅝ in)

270 mm
(10⅝ in)

622 mm
(24½ in)

517 mm
(20⅜ in)

22 mm
(⅞ in)

67 mm
(2⅝ in)

76 mm
(3 in)

48 mm (1⅞ in)
square section

22 mm
(⅞ in)

22 mm (⅞ in)

2541 mm
(92 in)

765 mm
(30⅛ in)

44 mm
(1¾ in)

22 mm
(⅞ in)

254 mm
(10 in)

1219 mm (48 in)
temporary tie

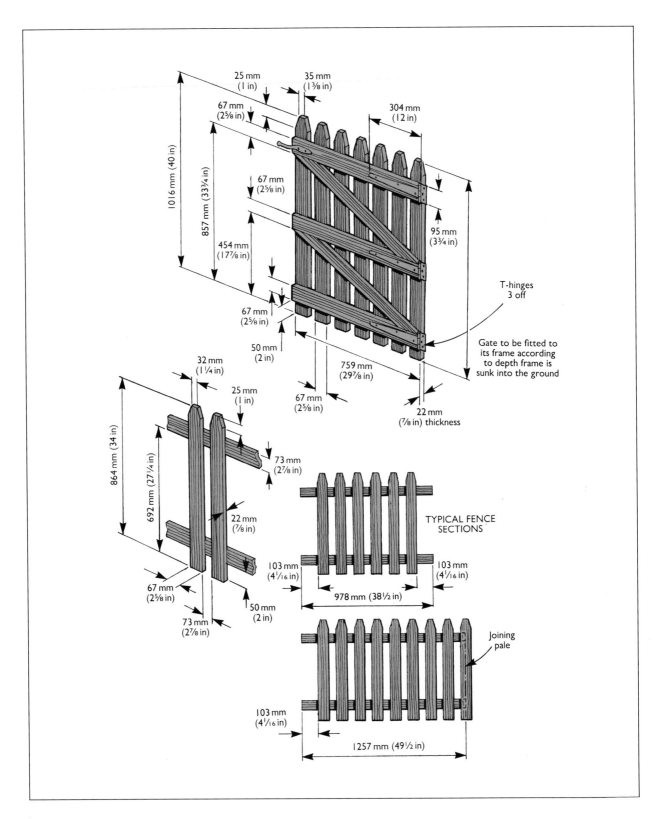

25 mm (1 in)

35 mm (1 3/8 in)

67 mm (2 5/8 in)

304 mm (12 in)

1016 mm (40 in)

857 mm (33 3/4 in)

67 mm (2 5/8 in)

95 mm (3 3/4 in)

454 mm (17 7/8 in)

67 mm (2 5/8 in)

50 mm (2 in)

759 mm (29 7/8 in)

67 mm (2 5/8 in)

22 mm (7/8 in) thickness

T-hinges 3 off

Gate to be fitted to its frame according to depth frame is sunk into the ground

32 mm (1 1/4 in)

25 mm (1 in)

864 mm (34 in)

692 mm (27 1/4 in)

73 mm (2 7/8 in)

22 mm (7/8 in)

67 mm (2 5/8 in)

73 mm (2 7/8 in)

50 mm (2 in)

TYPICAL FENCE SECTIONS

103 mm (4 1/16 in)

103 mm (4 1/16 in)

978 mm (38 1/2 in)

Joining pale

103 mm (4 1/16 in)

1257 mm (49 1/2 in)

– chipped some of the black paint off the rounded screw head. To prevent rust from instantly attacking this undefended spot, put a small drop of black paint on the head of each screw. Nothing – no, in my view absolutely nothing – looks worse than rusty screw heads on a new wooden gate.

Drill pilot holes and screw the hinges on to the gate first. Then, making sure that there is sufficient clearance in relation to both posts, fix the T-bars to the posts in the same way.

To keep the gate closed, fit a simple latch-type gate fastening.

## THE FENCE

Sections of fence are not difficult to make – much like an elongated gate, in fact, but with two horizontal rails rather than three. It is a good idea to decide first on the length of each section, and to cut the horizontal rails to length accordingly – but leaving a margin at each end in order to allow joints with other sections that can then be hidden behind vertical struts or posts.

**1** Cut the horizontal rails to length. Then clamp them together and mark with a pencil where the vertical struts are to be positioned. (But do not attach them yet.)

**2** Now shape the tops of the vertical struts. (The same pattern as the verticals of the gate would seem appropriate: see Step 3 of The Gate above.) Carefully glue and screw the first vertical strut on to the two horizontal rails (see Step 4 of The Gate above). Check for squareness before fixing on further struts. It may help construction to fix another vertical strut on at the far end of the section before attaching all the struts between.

## SETTING GATE- AND FENCE-POSTS INTO THE GROUND

There are several ways of fixing posts in the ground. Whatever method is chosen, however, it is vital that the lower ends of posts are soaked in wood preservative. Let them soak for at least 24 hours in a container of appropriate depth. The major danger area for the onset of rot is where the post enters the ground itself – not usually any deeper. Timber, after all, is generally long-lasting if there is a means for water to drain off its surface, above or below ground-level. It is at ground-level, especially if the post is con-creted in, that water most often accumulates. (Concrete even tends to hold water, effectively standing the post in a puddle.)

So, posts that are properly dug in together with hardcore packed tightly around them will last for a reasonable time. But this requires considerable time and effort in digging, setting up the posts, filling in, and finally making sure all are lined up correctly. (Any mistakes mean the immediate and inevitable duplication of all this hassle.)

Far better and simpler to use modern tech-nology in the form of the pre-formed steel socket with spiked tip. Available everywhere – although under different trade names – these sockets are the easy solution to all post fixing. The sockets come in all the principal sizes of commercially available wooden posts. They are initially hammered into the ground, as facilitated by the spiked tip (which is advertised to penetrate rapidly through even rock), and the posts are then simply slotted into them, the smaller sizes secured by screws driven through the sides. Each socket also has a drainage point so that water cannot become trapped. For set-ting posts up on paved or concrete surfaces, there are also bolt-on sockets in place of the spiked variety.

The two fence sections to be affixed to the fence posts are attached by screwing them onto the posts through their horizontals.

## FINISHING OFF

It is essential that the entire construction above ground is additionally treated with a good wood preservative.

> ### USEFUL TIP
> A fence can be made to look entirely different simply by changing the shape of the top of each slat. Experiment with a variety of cardboard shapes to get an individual look to your fence.

# PLANT TROUGH

A FEW WELL-MADE PLANT TROUGHS CAN MAKE DRIVEWAYS AND PORCHES LOOK SO MUCH MORE WELCOMING AND THE POSITIONING OF BRIGHT FLOWERS IN AND AROUND THE PLANT TROUGHS MAKES THE ENTIRE ASPECT OF THE HOUSE LOOK MUCH MORE INVITING.

The cost of a really attractive commercially-made trough can be prohibitive. If you are prepared to get down and make your own in wood, and to make more than one at a time (mass production), then you may even be able to construct six troughs for the cost of just one you can buy!

My construction method uses none of the more complex traditional joints: the dreaded mortice-and-tenon joint is avoided. The boarding is tongued and grooved – straight off the shelf of your nearest builder's merchant – so a big pot of waterproof glue, a quantity of zinc-plated Supascrews, and the usual hand tools are everything you need to be all set to go.

## STARTING OUT

**1** First, study the drawing. Then cut the four legs to length. At the bottom of each leg plane (or chisel) a chamfer on all four edges: this will prevent the wood from fraying and splitting if the trough is later dragged along the ground when full of soil.

**2** For this sort of operation a woodworker would traditionally use a mortice-and-tenon joint to attach the sides of the trough to the legs. In my design – to the relief of many, no doubt – I have instead introduced an intermediate stage. It involves battens of wood that are glued and screwed to the inside edges of the legs. (I have indicated the ideal size of batten in the Cutting List provided, but it is not critical – a little smaller or larger will do.) You need eight battens: two for each leg. Mark with a pencil on each leg where the battens are to be fixed. Once all the battens are glued to the legs, place this framework to one side and allow it sufficient standing time for the glue to cure (set). In the meanwhile turn your attention to the sides, which are in turn to be fixed to the battens.

**3** The sides and ends of the trough are all made from tongued-and-grooved boards. Basically, for our purposes, the wide V-moulding board is best. The V-machined groove gives a very pleasing line to the trough. Mark out all the sides and ends together: it is important that the boards are the same length, and that the ends are cut perfectly square.

## ASSEMBLING THE PARTS

**4** The tongued-and-grooved boards have now to be assembled, and screwed and glued on to the battens which have been glued to the legs. It is important to drill a pilot hole and to

**Any gravel drive or terrace will be enhanced by this Plant Trough full of colourful flowers. Raised off the floor, it has drainage holes in the base.**

BARBECUE SHELTER (PAGE 12),
WITH TRELLIS AND LADDER (PAGE 54)

BARBECUE CHAIR (PAGE 19)

TWO-SEATER BENCH (PAGE 28)

**TABLE AND BENCHES** (PAGE 22)

PERGOLA (PAGE 59)

LETTERBOX (PAGE 47)

ADIRONDACK-STYLE CHAIR (PAGE 42)

COMPOST BIN (PAGE 87)

PLANT TROUGH (PAGE 72)

TREE TROUGH (PAGE 76)

WINDOW BOX (PAGE 80)

OPEN FLOWER BARROW (PAGE 94)

**HIGH-SIDED FLOWER BARROW** (PAGE 94)

GARDEN GATE AND FENCE (PAGE 65)

NESTBOXES (PAGE 120)

OWL NESTBOX (PAGE 125)

SANDBOX AND LID (PAGE 106)

PLAY TOWER (PAGE 111)

BIRD TABLE (PAGE 128)

Corner post joints are used in several Projects in the book. Here, the corner blocks for the Plant

Trough are being fitted using a battery powered screwdriver.

## MATERIALS

Tongued-and-grooved
 boarding:
 V-machined (for the sides
  and ends)
 floorboards (for the base)
Wood for legs and battens
Thin boards or strips of
 wood (for the top frame
 of the trough)
Zinc-plated Supascrews
Wood preservative
(see Cutting List)

countersink the screw heads. Be generous with the glue when fixing the boards to the battens. It is normally easiest to fix the legs to the shorter lengths – the ends – first, and fix them all to the longer sides afterward. When the sides and ends are fixed, check again – before the glue cures – that the whole job is square.

The bottom of the trough is made from tongued-and-grooved floorboards. These differ from the boards you have just been handling in that their sides and edges are square.

The boards are now glued and screwed on to the sides and ends. It is important that the screws go into the centre of the side and end boards. To ensure that they do go into the right place, first pencil a line along the floorboards – it can save a lot of frustration!

The only potentially tricky bit is the cutting of a small section out of each board where the board has to fit around the legs. Place the board right next to the leg, and mark with a pencil the piece to be cut out. It is not difficult, but needs care to make a tidy job.

Now drill large drainage holes in the boards.

### FINISHING OFF

To finish off – and to give the trough a really clean line – boards or thin strips of wood may

## PLANT TROUGH CUTTING LIST

**Legs** 4 off 381 × 70 × 70 mm (15 × 2¾ × 2¾ in) timber

**Battens** 8 off 229 × 32 × 32 mm (9 × 1¼ × 1¼ in) timber

**Base** 3 off 794 × 152 × 22 mm (31¼ × 6 × ⅞ in) tongued-and-grooved floorboard

**Top frame** 2 off 876 × 89 × 16 mm (34½ × 3½ × ⅝ in) timber
2 off 540 × 89 × 16 mm (21¼ × 3½ × ⅝ in) timber

**Sides** 4 off 699 × 114 × 16 mm (27½ × 4½ × ⅝ in) V-grooved boarding

**Ends** 4 off 362 × 114 × 16 mm (14¼ × 4½ × ⅝ in) V-grooved boarding

be screwed to the top edges. In fact, those who want a really classic look might well prefer to add a mitred corner. For that, though, you will need a mitre-box to ensure a clean-cut joint. The square, butt-jointed ends look perfectly good enough, however, if you feel that you are not yet up to mitres. The boards or strips are glued and screwed on to the top of the trough.

It is essential that the wood is finally treated with a good wood preservative.

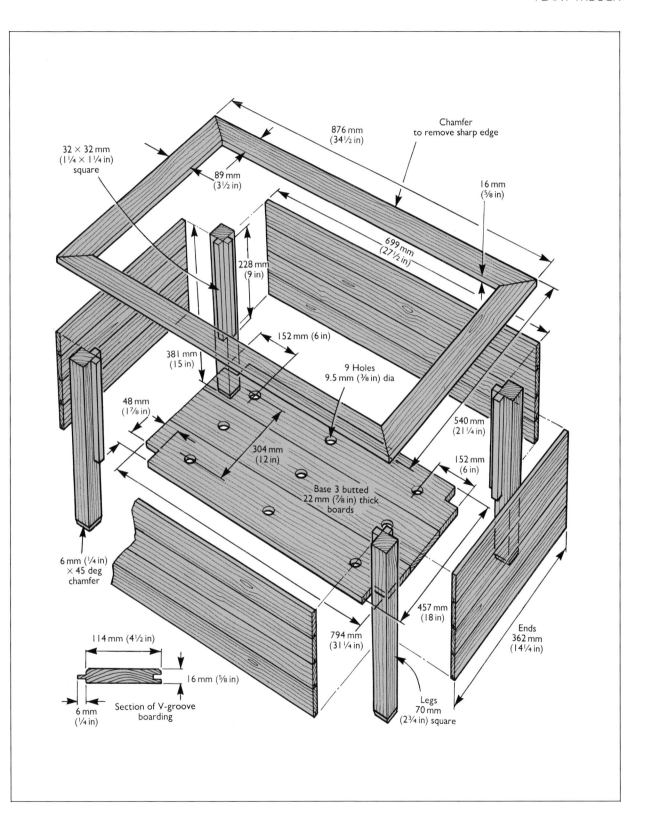

32 × 32 mm
(1¼ × 1¼ in)
square

89 mm
(3½ in)

876 mm
(34½ in)

Chamfer
to remove sharp edge

16 mm
(⅝ in)

228 mm
(9 in)

699 mm
(27½ in)

152 mm (6 in)

381 mm
(15 in)

9 Holes
9.5 mm (⅜ in) dia

48 mm
(1⅞ in)

540 mm
(21¼ in)

304 mm
(12 in)

152 mm
(6 in)

Base 3 butted
22 mm (⅞ in) thick
boards

6 mm (¼ in)
× 45 deg
chamfer

457 mm
(18 in)

Ends
362 mm
(14¼ in)

114 mm (4½ in)

16 mm (⅝ in)

6 mm
(¼ in)

Section of V-groove
boarding

794 mm
(31¼ in)

Legs
70 mm
(2¾ in) square

# TREE TROUGH

A VARIATION ON THE PLANT TROUGH (see page 72) IN DESIGN, BUT HAVING THE SAME BASIC CONSTRUCTION, IS THE LARGE SQUARE TROUGH OR BOX.

T his trough can be made to any size – but if you are hoping to plant a tree in it, then its dimensions must include room for the roots and space for enough soil around them to contain sufficient nutrients and moisture.

### STARTING OUT

**1** Study the drawings; in particular, compare them with the construction drawing of the Plant Trough. You will see that the construction method of both is really much the same.

Mark out, and cut the four legs to length. Pencil on all four legs (placed together for the purpose) exactly where the battens that will support the sides are to go. Once this is done, chamfer around the bottom of all four legs with a plane (or chisel) to prevent later fraying and splitting of the wood under stress.

**2** The top of the legs have to be shaped. This is not as difficult as it may at first seem, and there are several methods by which the shaping can be achieved.

- A coping saw can follow the curved line and produce a good finish. You will need a certain degree of patience as you work, however, or you may break the blade if you rush the cutting operation.
- The now oldfashioned bow saw can do the job quickly and efficiently.
- The modern counterpart of these two hand-saws is the electric jigsaw, which will certainly also do the job very speedily.

*Above:* Shaping the tops and chamfering the bottoms of the Tree Trough legs. Always chamfer the legs of any item made – it prevents the wood from splitting. Here, a spokeshave is used for chamfering, and a large, bevel-edged chisel is used to pare the bottoms of the legs.
*Right:* This square-shaped Tree Trough is ideal for a large flowering shrub or a conifer.

If you do not have any of these types of saw, you can still use a tenon saw or handsaw first to cut off the corners and then progressively to cut off the remaining angles. You will eventually be left with a series of jagged lines – but do not despair: use a *sharp* chisel and start to pare across the wood to remove them. Do not pare in one direction all the way across the leg, or the wood may tear out at the further edge. Pare up to half way, then turn the wood and work from the other side. It is really all so much easier than it sounds, and you should get a surprisingly good result. Finish off with glasspaper.

### ASSEMBLING THE PARTS

**3** The eight battens are now glued and screwed to the inner surfaces of the four legs. (Again compare the Plant Trough construction method.) Once all the battens are glued to the legs, place this framework to one side and allow it sufficient time for the glue to cure (set). Meanwhile turn your attention to the sides, which are in turn to be fixed to the battens.

**4** Tongued-and-grooved boards for the four sides of the trough should now be cut to length. Before cutting, check that you have accurately measured the length of the side and end boards: it is important that pairs of boards are the same length, and that the ends are cut perfectly square. Using glue and zinc-plated screws, fix the tongued-and-grooved boards to the battens and legs. Drill a pilot hole, and countersink the screw heads. Assemble all four sides.

**5** Once all four trough sides are glued together, it is vital to check for squareness. At this stage it is fairly easy to adjust the framework of panels, but when the glue is dry the whole structure will be immovably rigid. Use a sharp-pointed dowel rod to check for squareness. Place one end on any top corner of the frame, and rest the other end over the opposite top corner. Mark that corner with a pencil tick on the rod. Now position the rod diagonally over the remaining two

## TREE TROUGH CUTTING LIST

**Legs** 4 off 762 × 73 × 73 mm (30 × $2^7/_8$ × $2^7/_8$ in) timber

**Battens** 8 off 457 × 32 × 32 mm (18 × $1^1/_4$ × $1^1/_4$ in) timber

**Base** 6 off 591 × 114 × 19 mm ($23^1/_4$ × $4^1/_2$ × $3/_4$ in) tongued-and-grooved floorboards

**Top frame** 4 off 495 × 73 × 16 mm ($19^1/_2$ × $2^7/_8$ × $5/_8$ in) timber

**Sides** 16 off 495 × 114 × 16 mm ($19^1/_2$ × $4^1/_2$ × $5/_8$ in) V-grooved boarding

corners of the frame. If it is square, the position of the tick will match up between those two corners too. If necessary, place one side of the frame against the workbench and push the other side slightly but firmly to right or left as necessary. The frame will now be fairly heavy, so be careful when lifting it or moving it.

Once squareness is achieved, allow time for the glue to cure before turning the frame over and fitting the base.

**6** The base is made from tongued-and-grooved floorboards. Cutting small, square sections out of the boards so that they fit around the legs is the only potentially difficult bit. Place each board right next to the leg, and mark with a pencil the piece to be cut out. Then glue and screw the base boards on to the rest of the structure. Both methods of affixing are particularly important in relation to the base, for there will be a considerable weight on it when the trough is full of soil and plants.

Now drill holes in the boards to allow drainage.

### FINISHING OFF

Four strips of wood should additionally be glued and screwed around the top edges of the trough. This neatly rounds off the construction of the container. It is then essential that the wood is finally treated with a good wood preservative.

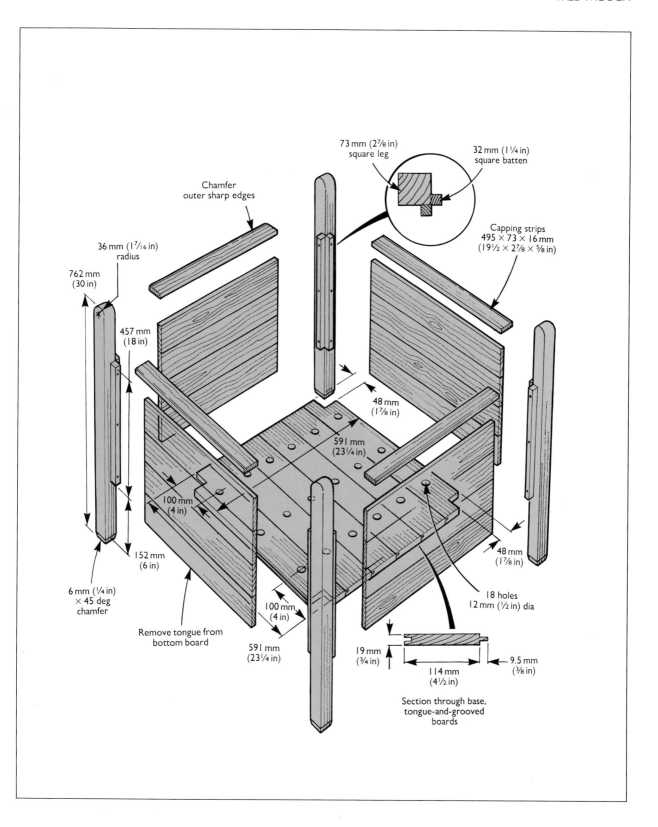

73 mm (2⁷⁄₈ in)
square leg

32 mm (1¹⁄₄ in)
square batten

Chamfer
outer sharp edges

Capping strips
495 × 73 × 16 mm
(19¹⁄₂ × 2⁷⁄₈ × ⁵⁄₈ in)

36 mm (1⁷⁄₁₆ in)
radius

762 mm
(30 in)

457 mm
(18 in)

48 mm
(1⁷⁄₈ in)

591 mm
(23¹⁄₄ in)

100 mm
(4 in)

152 mm
(6 in)

48 mm
(1⁷⁄₈ in)

6 mm (¹⁄₄ in)
× 45 deg
chamfer

18 holes
12 mm (¹⁄₂ in) dia

Remove tongue from
bottom board

100 mm
(4 in)

591 mm
(23¹⁄₄ in)

19 mm
(³⁄₄ in)

114 mm
(4¹⁄₂ in)

9.5 mm
(³⁄₈ in)

Section through base,
tongue-and-grooved
boards

# WINDOW BOX

A BEAUTIFUL BOX OF FLOWERS BENEATH A WINDOW IMPROVES THE APPEARANCE OF ANY HOUSE.

> TOOLS YOU WILL NEED
>
> 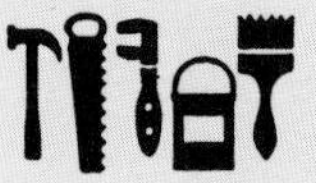
>
> A SHARP HANDSAW
> A COPING SAW *or* BOW SAW *or* JIGSAW
> A PENCIL
> A RULE OR MEASURE
> A SCREWDRIVER
> A DRILL
> bit for screws
> counterbore bit
> flat bit
> A PLUG CUTTER
> A PLANE
> A CHISEL
> A HAMMER
> WATERPROOF GLUE
> GLASSPAPER
> A LONG, SHARP-POINTED DOWEL ROD
> A CARPENTER'S KNIFE
> A COMPASS
> A PIECE OF PLAIN CARD

My design is intended to be simple to make but stylish to look at. Again I have avoided the more complicated traditional joints: corners in this window-box are glued and screwed. The decorative backboard can be simpler or – if you have the time – far more decorative than I have shown here: I have used ready-made mouldings that are available at a builder's merchant or DIY store and that can simply be glued on to the box. But such mouldings add a very attractive line, and the same sections of moulding can in any case be presented differently on your box to give an individual look to your work.

These days many houses have only narrow windowsills, so it is important that a window-box is self-supporting on the wall. The wall-brackets in my construction do require some shaping of the wood, to be sure, but again only glue and screws are used – no traditional joints.

## STARTING OUT

**1** First study the drawings and compare the Cutting List. Note that the front and back of the box are two lengths of timber which are cut to exactly the same length, and they are held together by two end pieces. As the width of the front board is different to that of the back board, it is necessary to cut the side pieces at an angle to ensure they fit.

Let's take those side pieces first. You could saw a plank perpendicularly to create a rectangle and then remove one corner to give the desired shape. But this would entail holding a comparatively short piece of wood while the more tricky cutting of the angle takes place. Far better (and potentially safer for fingers) to mark the angle on the plank with a pencil, cut the angle off – and then shorten the plank to the appropriate length with the perpendicular cut. Even better: use the same plank to make both side pieces.

Remove the roughness of the saw cuts afterward by using a jack plane. (It is attention to details like this that can give the box an almost professional finish.)

## ASSEMBLING THE PARTS

**2** The sides (ends) are glued and screwed to the horizontal lengths: butt jointed. The glue is waterproof glue, and the screw heads are to be counterbored to take 12 mm (3 in) wood plugs. In many garden projects it really does not matter if the countersunk holes (or even the screws themselves) are visible afterwards. In this particular job, however, holes would spoil the lines of the construction and it is worth going to some little expense to obtain a special tool known as a plug cutter. Now, a plug cutter's main function is to cut out a plug of wood of the exact diameter to fit in the counterbored hole and hide the screw head completely; moreover it hides it with wood of the correct tone and grain. (So

**Nothing looks more beautiful than a well-stocked Window Box. This one has a decorative board.**

many DIY woodworkers think that if a hole has to be filled, a piece of dowel rod will do. This, unfortunately, is not true, for the dowel rod is always visible as end grain in the surface grain of the plank.) From offcut wood of the right sort make as many plugs as you might possibly need. After chamfering around the edge of each plug, put a film of glue on the under side and hammer it into the hole over the screw head. If a plug snaps when hammered, it is not difficult to gouge out the remaining stump and insert a new one. Excess wood is pared off with a chisel when the glue has cured (set).

Glue, screw, and plug the whole window-box together, front, back and sides (ends).

## WINDOW BOX CUTTING LIST

**Sides (ends)** 2 off 286 × 222 × 22 mm (11¼ × 8¾ × ⅞ in) timber

**Back** 1 off 1226 × 222 × 22 mm (48¼ × 8¾ × ⅞ in) timber

**Front** 1 off 1226 × 149 × 22 mm (48¼ × 5⅞ × ⅞ in) timber

**Base** 1 off 1270 × 267 × 22 mm (50 × 10½ × ⅞ in) tongued-and-grooved floorboards

**Decorative board** 1 off 800 × 149 × 22 mm (31½ × 5⅞ × ⅞ in) timber

**Support brackets** 4 off 267 × 222 × 22 mm (10½ × 8¾ × ⅞ in) timber

## MATERIALS

Wood (for front, back and sides)

Tongued-and-grooved floorboards (for the base)

Board (for decorative back)

Ready-made mouldings

Wood (for brackets)

Posts (for uprights)

Zinc-plated Supascrews

Wood preservative

(see Cutting List)

Butt-jointing one piece of timber against another, to be fixed with glue and screws. To avoid the screw hole showing, the hole is counterbored and then a wood plug, cut with a plug cutter, is inserted. Any excess wood plug proud of the surface is trimmed off using a large chisel.

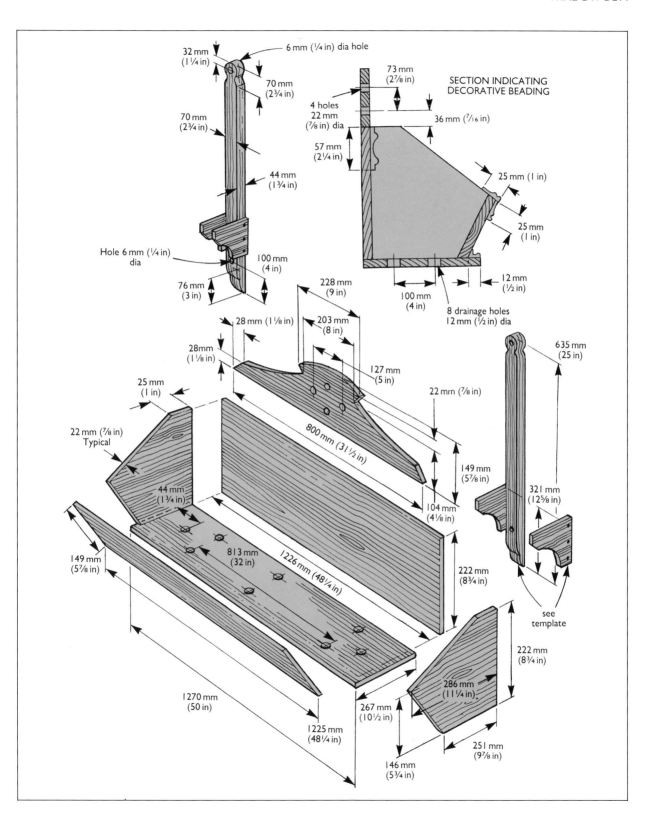

32 mm (1¼ in)

6 mm (¼ in) dia hole

70 mm (2¾ in)

70 mm (2¾ in)

44 mm (1¾ in)

Hole 6 mm (¼ in) dia

76 mm (3 in)

100 mm (4 in)

73 mm (2⅞ in)

SECTION INDICATING DECORATIVE BEADING

4 holes 22 mm (⅞ in) dia

36 mm (⁷⁄₁₆ in)

57 mm (2¼ in)

25 mm (1 in)

25 mm (1 in)

12 mm (½ in)

100 mm (4 in)

8 drainage holes 12 mm (½ in) dia

228 mm (9 in)

28 mm (1⅛ in)

203 mm (8 in)

28mm (1⅛ in)

25 mm (1 in)

127 mm (5 in)

22 mm (⁷⁄₈ in)

635 mm (25 in)

22 mm (⁷⁄₈ in) Typical

44 mm (1¾ in)

800 mm (31½ in)

149 mm (5⅞ in)

104 mm (4⅛ in)

321 mm (12⅝ in)

149 mm (5⅞ in)

813 mm (32 in)

1226 mm (48¼ in)

222 mm (8¾ in)

see template

222 mm (8¾ in)

1270 mm (50 in)

1225 mm (48¼ in)

267 mm (10½ in)

286 mm (11¼ in)

251 mm (9⅞ in)

146 mm (5¾ in)

83

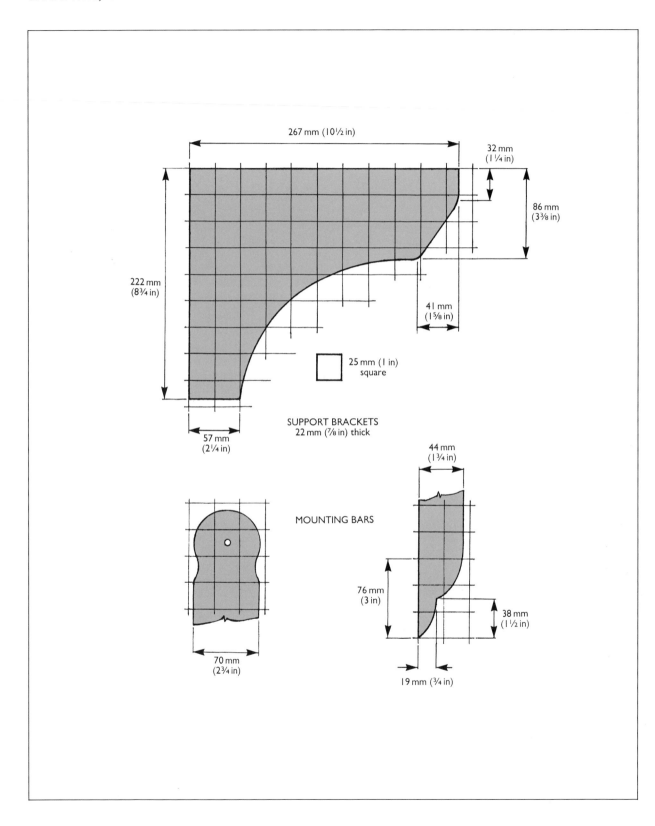

267 mm (10½ in)

32 mm
(1¼ in)

86 mm
(3⅜ in)

222 mm
(8¾ in)

41 mm
(1⅝ in)

25 mm (1 in)
square

SUPPORT BRACKETS
22 mm (⅞ in) thick

57 mm
(2¼ in)

MOUNTING BARS

44 mm
(1¾ in)

76 mm
(3 in)

38 mm
(1½ in)

70 mm
(2¾ in)

19 mm (¾ in)

Use a sharp-pointed dowel rod to check for squareness. Place one end on any top corner of the box, and rest the other end over the opposite top corner. Mark that corner with a pencil tick on the rod. Now position the rod diagonally over the remaining two corners of the box. If it is square, the position of the tick will match up between those two corners too.

**3** For the base, cut tongued-and-grooved floorboards to fit. If you prefer, you can use ordinary timber. In either case, however, drill

**This clearly shows the use of the mouldings which give this box its distinctive look. Note also the sturdy wooden brackets that support the box.**

drainage holes first, and use both glue and screws to attach the base to the front, back and sides (ends).

THE DECORATIVE BOARD
**4** How decorative you make the decorative board at the back is entirely up to you – but don't be too ambitious. Curves can be cut with

any of a variety of saws – by tradition the bow saw, for example, or in more recent times the coping saw. Wonderful work is possible with the coping saw, only the rule is not to push too hard as you work and always to have a pack of spare blades. An electric jigsaw, on the other hand, makes quick work of a job like this.

Before making decorative holes, make sure that you sketch out a proposed design first. The holes can be made with an electric drill and a flat bit. Even elongated slots can look good.

Take time and trouble afterward to remove all the roughness of the saw cuts with a plane or glasspaper.

**5** Before attaching the decorative board to the back with glue, use a carpenter's knife to make grooves in the receiving surface for the glue to "key" itself into. A hatching of knife lines provides extra adhesion area and thus makes for a stronger bond. Apply the glue to both surfaces; put the surfaces together and in position; and leave to cure. (The decorative board is not intended to bear any weight, so no further means of fixing is required.)

**6** Strips of ready-made moulding, apart from being quite fun to cut and apply, add a whole new dimension to the window-box and can make it look really very good. There is a vast range of shapes from which to choose, all of which should be on a chart at your local DIY store. The mouldings are glued on: industrial masking-tape can be used to retain pieces in position until the glue cures.

The window-box is now complete. All that remains now is to make the brackets that fix it to the wall.

## FIXING THE WINDOW-BOX

**7** The easiest way to fix a window-box to the wall would be to use metal wall-brackets. But if you have come this far, why not go the whole hog and make what should turn out to be a good-looking set of wooden wall-brackets?

Mark out the two verticals. Use a compass to scribe the radius at the top. To reproduce the shaping at the bottom, mark the design on a piece of card, cut it out, and use it as a template to redraw the shape on the wood. Cut the shape with a bow saw, a coping saw or a jigsaw. Afterward, remove the rough saw cuts with glasspaper.

**8** Now cut out the brackets themselves, remembering to try to keep the grain running in a horizontal direction; if the grain is not horizontal, the brackets might split and sheer when in use. Drill pilot holes that are counterbored for the screws. Glue and screw the brackets to the upright posts. Take care to align the brackets before the final screws are driven home. Hammer and glue wood plugs into the counterbored holes; any that remain proud can be cut down flush with a sharp chisel.

Now drill holes at the top and bottom of the uprights to take the screws that will affix them to the wall.

**9** Fix the brackets on to the window-box with screws that pass through the base. A couple of screws should also be driven through the back of the box to fix the uprights to the box.

## FINISHING OFF

It is essential that the wood is finally treated with a good wood preservative.

# COMPOST BIN

BINS OR CONTAINERS IN WHICH TO DEPOSIT GARDEN OR HOUSEHOLD GREEN WASTE ABOUND IN A VARIETY OF SHAPES AND SIZES. SOME OF THE LARGER PLASTIC BINS AVAILABLE IN GARDEN CENTRES AND DIY STORES LOOK LIKE OVERGROWN MUSHROOMS. BUT FEW COMBINE THE ESSENTIAL FACTORS OF LARGE CAPACITY, TIDY LOOKS, READY ACCESS FOR GETTING THE COMPOST OUT, AND MINIMUM COST. SO I THOUGHT I'D MAKE MY OWN.

Hard to believe, but some commercially available bins really don't provide any means of getting the compost out other than by dismantling the bin altogether. And this despite the fact that compost bins are big business at the garden stores at present.

My big big bin has a trap door in it that is quite definitely large enough for its owner to take a fair-sized shovelful of compost out whenever necessary. As for the overall cost of construction, I used a combination of plywood and batten to keep the expense right down.

## STARTING OUT

**I** First, study the diagrams and the Cutting List. With these in mind, you will have a good idea of what is required when you go to purchase your sheet of plywood.

One of the cheapest types of plywood available is the variety used in the building industry for shuttering concrete. Plywood for shuttering has one processed (smooth) side and, normally, one rough side. It is technically graded "W.P.B.", which means that it is suitable for use in the open air in all weather conditions, and when wet should not separate into its individual layers

of ply. It is entirely appropriate to this project – cheap and effective – and forms the main four sides of my bin.

**2** A sheet of plywood usually measures 8 feet by 4 feet (or its metric equivalent: 2.44 × 1.22 metres). Take a ruler and a pencil and mark the sheet in four equal rectangular parts – which gives you four pieces of 4 ft × 2 ft (1.22 m × 61 cm).

Cut them out. It is best to use a fine-toothed handsaw for cutting plywood: a saw with larger teeth may fray the edges of the plywood as it cuts, and if you were not very careful you could harm yourself nastily on splinters.

The top of the bin is to be sloped, to prevent water from collecting on the lid. This means the two sides have to have an angle cut on them, and a thin rectangular piece must be cut from the top of the front. Clamp the sides together to cut them equally and simultaneously. Consult the diagram for the angle, and for the dimensions of the piece to be taken off the front.

**3** The next task is to cut the trap door in the front. Consult the diagram, and pencil in the trap door on the front piece. Use a jigsaw to cut it out, making as sharp a right-angle as possible

each side at the top of the door without taking the jigsaw from the wood. Once the door is separated from the front piece, use a piece of glasspaper to smooth down any rough edges on door or front.

### ASSEMBLING THE PARTS

**4** A piece of batten now has to be glued and screwed horizontally across the top of the trap door on the front piece, and two other battens vertically down each side of the door itself. A light coating of waterproof glue on adjoining surfaces should suffice. There should be no need to drill pilot holes for the short zinc-plated screws. The battens have two purposes: to lend strength to the plywood, and to provide good fixing for the hinges.

**5** Hinges for the trap door should be of the japanned (black) T-shaped variety, which are simply screwed into the supporting battens — a far simpler type of hinge than ordinarily used in carpentry or cabinet-making. Use the

*Above:* The sloping lid prevents rain from cooling down the compost, and the T-strap hinges and bolts keep the door firmly closed. The use of cranked bolts makes it impossible for them to go over the battens on the door.
*Right:* With most Compost Bins it is difficult to get the compost out. This bin avoids such problems as compost is removed through the trap door.

black-topped round-headed screws that come with them.

To hold the door shut when the bin is full, a bolt should be fitted to the front on each side of the door. The type of bolt required is one that has a double right-angle (a crank) at the operative end; the cranked portion of the bolt allows it to fit over the batten on the side of the door, keeping it firmly closed.

**6** Now glue and screw battens to the inside vertical edges of the bin sides. As before, put a thin coating of glue on adjoining surfaces, but you may find it easier this time to drill pilot holes first before you drive the zinc-plated screws through into the plywood.

## MATERIALS

MATERIALS

Wood:

   plywood external-grade
     sheet

   plywood offcut (for the
     floor)

   tongued-and-grooved
     boarding (for the lid,
     and possibly for the
     floor)

   battens (of various sizes)

   dowel rods

Zinc-plated Supascrews

Japanned (black) T-hinges
   and black-topped round-
   headed screws

Two crank-headed fastening
   bolts

Three cup hooks

Two screw eyes

Nylon cord

Elastic expanding baggage
   strap

(Two catches, to hold the
   lid down)

Water-based wood
   preservative

(Expanded polystyrene
   sheet)

(see Cutting List)

Begin to assemble the bin. Attach one of the sides to the back, again with both glue and screws. And attach the other side to the front, also with glue and screws. Finally bring the two halves together and fix them solidly, once more with glue and screws.

While the glue is still moist, make sure that this framework of the bin is square. A good method for doing this is to place a thin batten or short length of dowel diagonally across from one corner to the opposite corner, mark on the batten or dowel where the edges of the corners meet, and then place the same piece across the other corners diagonally, checking that the marks meet in exactly the same place. If they don't, gently force the sides one way or another until they do.

**7** Next, glue and screw battens to the top and bottom inner edges of the bin frame. Apart from anything else, these battens will facilitate the fixing on of a floor to the bin – if a floor is required at all.

Many compost bins are open to the ground (which thus provides a means of drainage). My box, however, is designed to be portable and ordinarily to stand on a concrete surface – which is why I have given it a solid base. But if you have a specific fixed site for the bin in the garden, it is perfectly feasible not to have a floor: all you need to remember is to ensure that there is provision for the trap door to open freely, uncluttered by soil or stones.

The floor itself is made either from the same type of plywood as the sides – it should be possible to buy an offcut of suitable size – or from tongued-and-grooved floorboarding. It is fixed into place with screws that pass through the underside into the battens and sides of the box frame. Because in the compost there will inevitably be liquid that seeps down to the bottom, drill some large holes in the floor to allow it to escape, and raise the floor off the

## COMPOST BIN CUTTING LIST

**Front** 1 off 1057 × 610 × 12 mm (41⅝ × 24 × ½ in) plywood

2 off 1063 × 41 × 22 mm (41⅞ × 1⅝ × ⅞ in) timber

1 off 502 × 41 × 22 mm (19¾ × 1⅝ × ⅞ in) timber

2 off 73 × 41 × 22 mm (2⅞ × 1⅝ × ⅞ in) timber

1 off 610 × 35 × 22 mm (24 × 1⅜ × ⅞ in) timber

**Back** 1 off 1220 × 610 × 12 mm (48 × 24 × ½ in) plywood

2 off 1220 × 41 × 22 mm (48 × 1⅝ × ⅞ in) timber

2 off 502 × 41 × 22 mm (19¾ × 1⅝ × ⅞ in) timber

**Sides** 2 off 1220 × 610 × 12 mm (48 × 24 × ½ in) plywood

2 off 565 × 41 × 22 mm (22¼ × 1⅝ × ⅞ in) timber

2 off 610 × 57 × 22 mm (24 × 2¼ × ⅞ in) timber

**Floor** 1 off 610 × 610 × 22 mm (24 × 24 × ½ in) plywood or tongued-and-grooved boarding

3 off 635 × 44 × 44 mm (25 × 1¾ × 1¾ in) timber

**Trap door** 1 off 350 × 250 × 12 mm (13¾ × 9⅞ × ½ in) plywood

1 off 343 × 35 × 22 mm (13½ × 1⅜ × ⅞ in) timber

2 off 250 × 35 × 22 mm (9⅞ × 1⅜ × ⅞ in) timber

1 off 25 mm diam. × 111 mm length (1 in diam. × 4⅜ in length) dowel

**Lid** 2 off 708 × 35 × 22 mm (27⅞ × 1⅜ × ⅞ in) timber

2 off 667 × 35 × 22 mm (26¼ × 1⅜ × ⅞ in) timber

8 off 762 × 89 × 16 mm (30 × 3½ × ⅝ in) match boarding

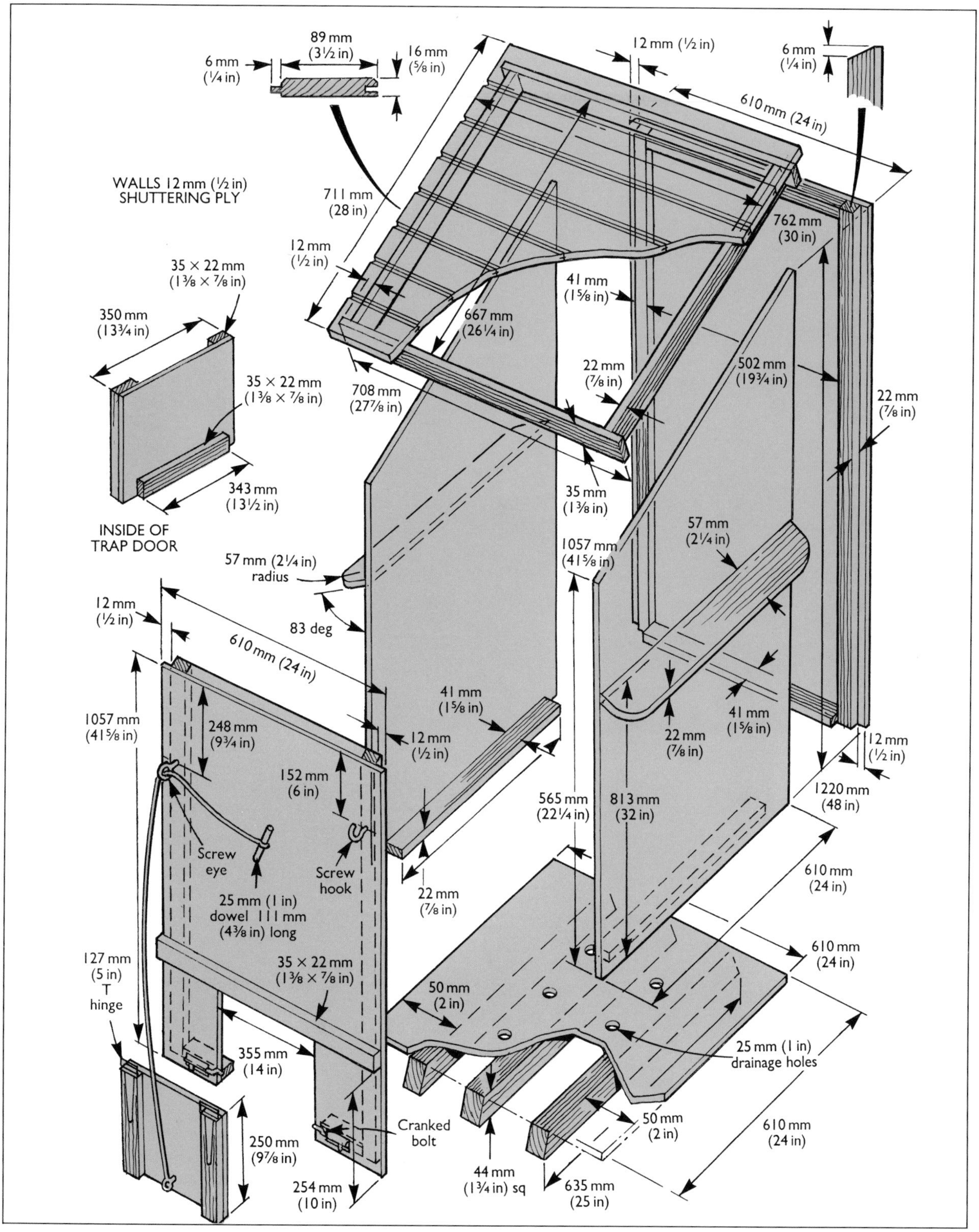

89 mm (3½ in)
6 mm (¼ in)
16 mm (⅝ in)
12 mm (½ in)
6 mm (¼ in)
610 mm (24 in)
WALLS 12 mm (½ in) SHUTTERING PLY
711 mm (28 in)
12 mm (½ in)
762 mm (30 in)
35 × 22 mm (1⅜ × ⅞ in)
41 mm (1⅝ in)
350 mm (13¾ in)
667 mm (26¼ in)
35 × 22 mm (1⅜ × ⅞ in)
708 mm (27⅞ in)
22 mm (⅞ in)
502 mm (19¾ in)
22 mm (⅞ in)
343 mm (13½ in)
35 mm (1⅜ in)
INSIDE OF TRAP DOOR
57 mm (2¼ in) radius
1057 mm (41⅝ in)
57 mm (2¼ in)
12 mm (½ in)
83 deg
610 mm (24 in)
41 mm (1⅝ in)
41 mm (1⅝ in)
1057 mm (41⅝ in)
248 mm (9¾ in)
12 mm (½ in)
22 mm (⅞ in)
12 mm (½ in)
152 mm (6 in)
565 mm (22¼ in)
813 mm (32 in)
1220 mm (48 in)
Screw eye
Screw hook
25 mm (1 in) dowel 111 mm (4⅜ in) long
22 mm (⅞ in)
610 mm (24 in)
127 mm (5 in) T hinge
35 × 22 mm (1⅜ × ⅞ in)
610 mm (24 in)
50 mm (2 in)
355 mm (14 in)
25 mm (1 in) drainage holes
Cranked bolt
250 mm (9⅞ in)
50 mm (2 in)
610 mm (24 in)
44 mm (1¾ in) sq
254 mm (10 in)
635 mm (25 in)

ground a little with three parallel battens.

**8** A portable bin must have handles – and if they are to be fixed on from the inside, it is much easier to do so while there is still no lid. Even if the bin is to have no base and live on a fixed site, it may be useful to have handles to lift the thing up from time to time.

The handles are simply pieces of batten glued and screwed on to the sides of the bin. But they should be shaped first: plane an angle along the top edge of each handle to make sure that rain will drain off freely. The angle is not critical, but it should be there. Once more, coat with glue adjoining surfaces and (probably after drilling pilot holes) screw in the battens from the inside of the bin. The screws should be long and fairly large – 5 cm (2 in) long, say, and 4 mm (⅙ in, No. 10) in diameter – use six screws for each handle.

*Above:* Most Compost Bins sit flat on the ground; this one is designed to be moved, hence the base has holes drilled to let liquid escape. It also has battens underneath to allow the base to dry off. Timber subject to damp which never has time to dry will quickly rot.
*Top right:* The pull-cord handle and hook eye make it possible for the door to stay in the "open" position while the compost is shovelled out.
*Bottom right:* With the bolts withdrawn and the door pulled up, there is plenty of room for a shovel to get in at the compost.

**9** The lid has to be strong to keep out the cold and the rain, and must also prevent the drying effects of wind and sun. To keep the rain off the bin as much as possible, the lid should also overhang the sides by a fair margin. For its composition I recommend decorative tongued-and-grooved boarding: the boards can be held rigidly together by battens which are glued and screwed on, and positioned (for extra insulation) to fit just within the battens at the top of the four sides of the bin.

For ordinary purposes, all you need to keep the lid on the bin is an elastic baggage strap slung across the top between two cup hooks, one screwed into each side of the bin. If you live in a windy area, you may have to devise some less casual method of keeping the lid on. You could, for example, fit a couple of catches under the overhang on each side of the bin.

**10** To keep the trap door open while you shovel compost out, fit a hook screw eye at the bottom of the door, another towards the top of the front of the bin on one side, and a third at the same height but on the other side of the front of the bin.

Now attach a piece of nylon cord to the eye at the bottom of the door, and thread it up through the eye towards the top of the front of the bin. Drill a hole through the length of a short piece of dowel rod, and thread the nylon cord through the hole, knotting it at the top end so that the dowel rod becomes a handle on the string. With a little trial and error on the length of the nylon cord and on pulling it to open the door, the dowel rod can be made to catch on the cup hook opposite the eye on the front of the bin, and so hold open the door.

FINISHING OFF

If you use a wood preservative to protect the bin, make sure it is a water-based one. There are some very suitable preservatives available, some advertised in addition not to harm plants nor poison family pets.

The best bins have good insulation. Wood retains heat naturally, and the plywood used here should also prevent moisture loss. But you might like in addition to line the interior walls with expanded polystyrene. Alternatively, strips of old carpet can be used to line bins, but in time become rather messy.

Experience with your bin in use will indicate whether on the other hand more aeration is needed. If it is, drill a few holes in the sides.

# FLOWER BARROWS

WHEN THE OLD-STYLE WOODEN WHEELBARROW WAS ABANDONED IN FAVOUR OF THE ALL-STEEL RUBBER-WHEELED STACKABLE VARIETY, IT WAS NOT LONG BEFORE ENTERPRISING GARDENERS WITH AN EYE FOR BEAUTY BEGAN TO USE THE OLD BARROWS AS CONTAINERS FOR DISPLAYS OF FLOWERS.

## TOOLS YOU WILL NEED

A SAW
A TENON SAW
A COPING SAW *or*
A JIGSAW
A PENCIL
A RULE OR MEASURE
A SCREWDRIVER
A DRILL
bit for screws
flat bit
A SMOOTHING PLANE
(A JACK PLANE)
WATERPROOF GLUE
CLAMPS/SASH CRAMPS
A CARPENTER'S KNIFE
GLASSPAPER
A SPOKESHAVE
A PIECE OF PLAIN CARD
A COMPASS
A PROTRACTOR
BLOCKS OF WOOD
(for support)
A SLIDING BEVEL GAUGE

Today, most of the traditional wooden barrows have rotted away – but the simple, graceful lines of the old wooden garden implements have not lost their appeal. That is why I have here tried to recapture the graceful lines of a wooden barrow, right down to a very simplified wooden wheel.

But first a warning to those who are new to woodworking projects: *this is certainly not a good one to start on*. The barrow's construction may look relatively simple at first, but – as I found out myself in due course – there are many different angles that have to be cut, and in woodwork the cutting of angles invariably spells problems for even the most experienced of woodworkers.

In an effort to strike upon a compromise, I actually made two barrows, one – the open type – of much more simple design than the traditional high-sided type. If you decide to have a go at making either type, be prepared to take both time and care – but the result will be something to stand back and enjoy.

### STARTING OUT

**1** First study the drawings. Compare the two types of barrow and decide which is the one you would rather make. Both barrows have much in common, especially in the basic components: the chassis, the legs, the wheels,

the axle blocks, and the leg support brackets. Other parts, however, are utterly different, especially the sides.

Begin construction by cutting to length the handle-struts that form a chassis for the base. Then trace out the shape of one of the handles on a plain card, cut out the shape, and use it as a template to transfer the outline on to the handle-strut. Actually cutting the shape in the wood does involve cutting curves, I know, and may therefore strike the inexperienced with a measure of doubt but the right tool for the job should make the whole thing relatively painless. The simplest tool for cutting curves is the coping saw – which indeed copes very well in cutting out this outline and for all the other curved brackets and sides that this project requires. An electric jigsaw, however (if you have one), will do the job far more speedily.

When both handles are cut out, wrap a piece of glasspaper around a cylindrical offcut (such as a dowel rod) and use it to glasspaper smooth both handholds.

**2** The next task is to glue and screw battens on the inside edges of each handle-strut. The base of the barrow itself is to be constructed of tongued-and-grooved floorboard: the thick-

**This Flower Barrow will brighten up any corner. The wooden wheel makes it look very rustic.**

ness of the board is significant, for the battens have to be glued on to the handle-strut sides in such a way as to allow the top of the boards to be parallel with the top of the handle-struts. It is therefore advisable to gauge the dimensions you need from the board you have.

A HIGH-SIDED OR AN OPEN BARROW?
**3** Constructing the barrow base is where the difference between the two barrows begins to impinge on the construction method. The overall width of the floorboards used as the base in each barrow is not identical. The open barrow is squarer in form; the high-sided barrow is more pointed in shape. But neither is

The Flower Barrows have wooden brackets to support the framework. Use a coping saw to cut these brackets.

## MATERIALS
Wood:
  planks
  tongued-and-grooved
    boards
  battens
  dowel rods
Zinc-plated Supascrews
Candle wax/grease
Wood preservative
(see Cutting List)

## FLOWER BARROW CUTTING LIST
### OPEN BARROW
**Main frame** 2 off 902 × 51 × 32 mm (35½ × 2 × 1¼ in) timber

**(Handle-struts)** 2 off 397 × 35 × 22 mm (15⅝ × 1⅜ × ⅞ in) timber

**Barrow base** 4 off 432 × 114 × 16 mm (17 × 4½ × ⅝ in) tongued-and-grooved board

**Leg** 2 off 311 × 44 × 44 mm (12¼ × 1¾ × 1¾ in) timber

**Leg bracket** 2 off 133 × 114 × 19 mm (5¼ × 4½ × ¾ in) timber

**Wheel** 1 off 216 × 216 × 22 mm (8½ × 8½ × ⅞ in) timber
2 off 216 × 35 × 22 mm (8½ × 1⅜ × ⅞ in) timber
1 off 16 mm diam. × 384 mm length (⅝ in diam. × 15⅛ in length) dowel

**Axle block** 2 off 108 × 54 × 22 mm (4¼ × 2⅛ × ⅞ in) timber

**Front support** 4 off 419 × 114 × 16 mm (16½ × 4½ × ⅝ in) tongued-and-grooved floorboard
2 off 419 × 32 × 22 mm (16½ × 1¼ × ⅞ in) timber

**Rear support** 1 off 495 × 95 × 16 mm (19½ × 3¾ × ⅝ in) tongued-and-grooved floorboard

**Front support bracket** 2 off 152 × 159 × 19 mm (6 × 6¼ × ¾ in) timber

### HIGH-SIDED BARROW
**Main frame** 2 off 902 × 51 × 32 mm (35½ × 2 × 1¼ in) timber

**(Handle-struts)** 2 off 397 × 29 × 22 mm (15⅝ × 1⅛ × ⅞ in) timber

**Barrow base** 4 off 464 × 114 × 16 mm (18¼ × 4½ × ⅝ in) tongued-and-grooved board

**Leg** 2 off 311 × 44 × 44 mm (12¼ × 1¾ × 1¾ in) timber

**Leg bracket** 2 off 135 × 111 × 19 mm (5⁵⁄₁₆ × 4⅜ × ¾ in) timber

**Wheel** 1 off 216 × 216 × 22 mm (8½ × 8½ × ⅞ in) timber
2 off 216 × 35 × 22 mm (8½ × 1⅜ × ⅞ in) timber
1 off 16 mm diam. × 263 mm length (⅝ in diam. × 10⅜ in length) dowel

**Axle block** 2 off 108 × 54 × 22 mm (4¼ × 2⅛ × ⅞ in) timber

**Front wall** 3 off 470 × 152 × 22 mm (18½ × 6 × ⅞ in) tongued-and-grooved floorboard

**Side wall** 4 off 603 × 152 × 22 mm (23¾ × 6 × ⅞ in) tongued-and-grooved floorboard

**Rear wall** 1 off 587 × 152 × 22 mm (23⅛ × 6 × ⅞ in) tongued-and-grooved floorboard

**Front wall bracket** 2 off 168 × 148 × 19 mm (6⅝ × 5¾ × ¾ in) timber

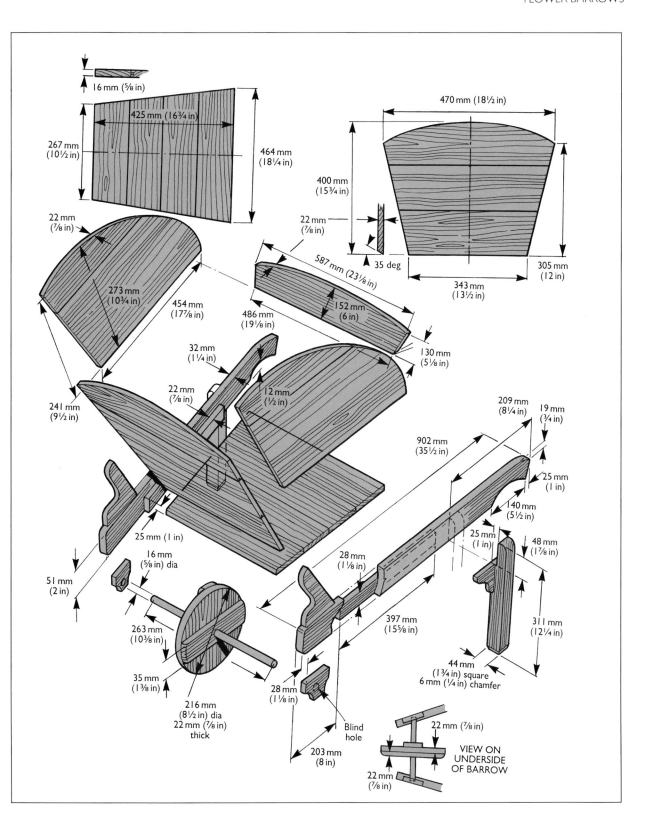

16 mm (⁵⁄₈ in)

425 mm (16¾ in)

267 mm (10½ in)

464 mm (18¼ in)

470 mm (18½ in)

400 mm (15¾ in)

22 mm (⁷⁄₈ in)

35 deg

305 mm (12 in)

343 mm (13½ in)

22 mm (⁷⁄₈ in)

273 mm (10¾ in)

454 mm (17⁷⁄₈ in)

587 mm (23⅛ in)

152 mm (6 in)

486 mm (19⅛ in)

130 mm (5⅛ in)

241 mm (9½ in)

32 mm (1¼ in)

22 mm (⁷⁄₈ in)

12 mm (½ in)

209 mm (8¼ in)

19 mm (¾ in)

902 mm (35½ in)

25 mm (1 in)

140 mm (5½ in)

25 mm (1 in)

48 mm (1⁷⁄₈ in)

51 mm (2 in)

16 mm (⁵⁄₈ in) dia

28 mm (1⅛ in)

25 mm (1 in)

263 mm (10⅜ in)

397 mm (15⅝ in)

311 mm (12¼ in)

35 mm (1⅜ in)

44 mm (1¾ in) square 6 mm (¼ in) chamfer

216 mm (8½ in) dia 22 mm (⁷⁄₈ in) thick

28 mm (1⅛ in)

Blind hole

203 mm (8 in)

22 mm (⁷⁄₈ in)

22 mm (⁷⁄₈ in)

VIEW ON UNDERSIDE OF BARROW

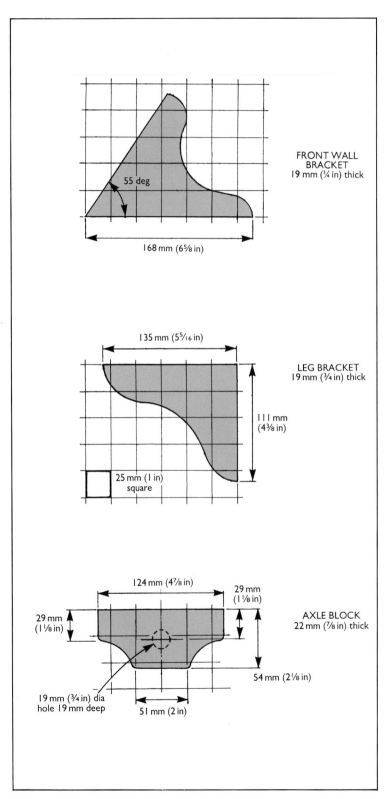

FRONT WALL
BRACKET
19 mm (¾ in) thick

55 deg

168 mm (6⅝ in)

135 mm (5⁵⁄₁₆ in)

LEG BRACKET
19 mm (¾ in) thick

111 mm
(4⅜ in)

25 mm (1 in)
square

124 mm (4⅞ in)

29 mm
(1⅛ in)

29 mm
(1⅛ in)

AXLE BLOCK
22 mm (⅞ in) thick

54 mm (2⅛ in)

19 mm (¾ in) dia
hole 19 mm deep

51 mm (2 in)

actually square, and both thus require an angle to be cut across the ends of the boards. Probably the simplest way to achieve this angle is first to cut the boards to slightly more than the right rectangular length. With a protractor and a straight edge, mark out the angle across the ends in pencil. Cut the ends off: by doing so you will in fact be cutting off the tongue across one end, and the groove across the other, so leaving you at both ends with a square-ended board and nowhere for water to collect.

Glue and screw the cut base pieces of floorboard on to the battens already fixed to the handle-strut sides.

**4** The sides and the front of the high-sided barrow are too wide to be made out of a single board. Planks have to be glued together. Gluing planks together is not difficult, but there is a certain method to it that ensures strong and permanent adhesion.

*Method:* First check the edge of the board for squareness and flatness. The easiest way to do this is to place the board on top of another board: if one rocks up and down, you have a high spot which will have to be planed down. To locate the high spot, bring the boards up to eye level and check along the junction. The plane

Using a smoothing plane with the aid of a square wood block to keep the plane horizontal. When planks have to be jointed it is important that the edges to be joined are flat and are at right angles. The smoothing plane helps with this job.

used should ideally be a jack plane, which has a longer sole than a smoothing plane and so removes high spots more simply.

A useful tip is to position a square block of wood beneath the plane as you line up the edge of the board – the block will keep your plane perfectly horizontal while supporting the sole as you move along the board. Keep the block tight against the side of the plane and the side of the board.

When all high spots have been planed flat, the edges that are to be glued together have to be "keyed": use a carpenter's knife (with a new blade) to carve a pattern of grooves criss-crossing the edges. This increases the gluing surface and thus strengthens the bond. Modern glues are so effective that keying in this fashion makes the joint stronger than the wood itself. Use waterproof glue. Paste it on both surfaces to be joined, and when bringing the edges together, rub them together a little to make sure that the glue is impregnated well into the

**The "Sack" Barrow is a thing of the past. Although it has the same basic chassis as the Flower Barrow it is simpler to make. Filled with flowers it makes an attractive addition to the garden.**

wood. A pair of sash cramps should be used to retain the wood in position while the glue cures (sets): if you don't have any, they can be obtained from tool hire shops.

This method of jointing planks together is eminently suitable for gardening projects. The real secret is first to make sure that the edges to be joined are flat and square.

**5** The front and back pieces of the open barrow are much simpler still. The front of the barrow is made of tongued-and-grooved boards held together by two battens glued and screwed to the back of the boards. Before attaching the front to the barrow, the top board should be shaped. Cut the tongue or groove off before cutting the curve. The smaller back piece is similarly shaped, and glued and screwed from the under side to the barrow.

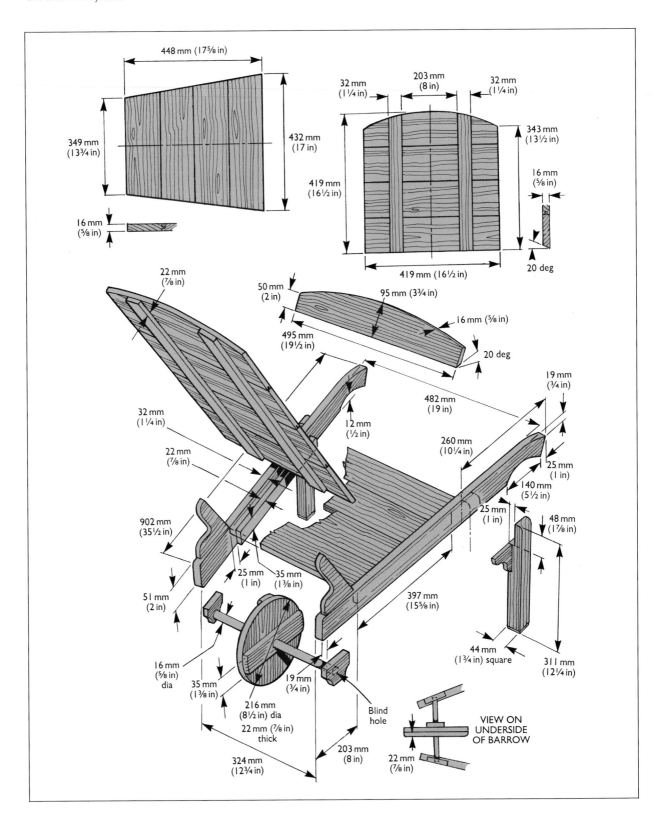

448 mm (17⅝ in)

349 mm (13¾ in)

432 mm (17 in)

16 mm (⅝ in)

32 mm (1¼ in)

203 mm (8 in)

32 mm (1¼ in)

343 mm (13½ in)

419 mm (16½ in)

16 mm (⅝ in)

419 mm (16½ in)

20 deg

22 mm (⅞ in)

50 mm (2 in)

95 mm (3¾ in)

16 mm (⅝ in)

495 mm (19½ in)

20 deg

482 mm (19 in)

19 mm (¾ in)

260 mm (10¼ in)

25 mm (1 in)

140 mm (5½ in)

32 mm (1¼ in)

12 mm (½ in)

22 mm (⅞ in)

25 mm (1 in)

48 mm (1⅞ in)

902 mm (35½ in)

51 mm (2 in)

25 mm (1 in)

35 mm (1⅜ in)

397 mm (15⅝ in)

44 mm (1¾ in) square

311 mm (12¼ in)

16 mm (⅝ in) dia

35 mm (1⅜ in)

216 mm (8½ in) dia
22 mm (⅞ in) thick

19 mm (¾ in)

Blind hole

203 mm (8 in)

324 mm (12¾ in)

22 mm (⅞ in)

VIEW ON UNDERSIDE OF BARROW

**6** The front of the open barrow has wooden brackets that support it. Use a coping saw to cut out the brackets and then remove the rough saw cuts (and ensure that edges are rounded) with glasspaper.

Put the front up against the barrow and, with an extra pair of hands to help, mark in pencil where the brackets fit. Now drill holes in the brackets to take the screws that will hold bracket, front, and handle-strut together. Glue the front to the barrow along the bottom edge. The brackets are then glued to the front and the handle-struts, and the screws are driven in. (It is important at this stage to get a helper to hold the front in place while you deal with the brackets, glue and screws.)

The small sill at the back is now easily attached.

**7** Cutting and planing the angles on the bottom of the sides of the high-sided barrow requires more concentration, perhaps even more skill, but above all, more patience. Try to think it all through before doing it – whatever you do, don't rush it – and the chances are that you will achieve a good result.

First, cut the front of the barrow to shape. An angle has to be planed off the bottom edge so that the whole front tilts forward.

*Method:* Transfer the angle from the diagram to the wood by marking the appropriate gradient on the ends. (An instrument called a sliding bevel gauge is useful for this operation, although it is not imperative to get hold of one.) Then draw a line along the full length of the front at the edge of where the angle is to be. With a plane, and taking full-length strokes, plane the corner of the wood down to the line, checking also the angled lines at the end as a reference to ensure an even edge. The more consistently you manage planing whole lengths at a time across the wood, the more even the resulting edge is likely to be. It is not really difficult, but if you are not confident of being able to do it the first time, practise on a length of batten beforehand.

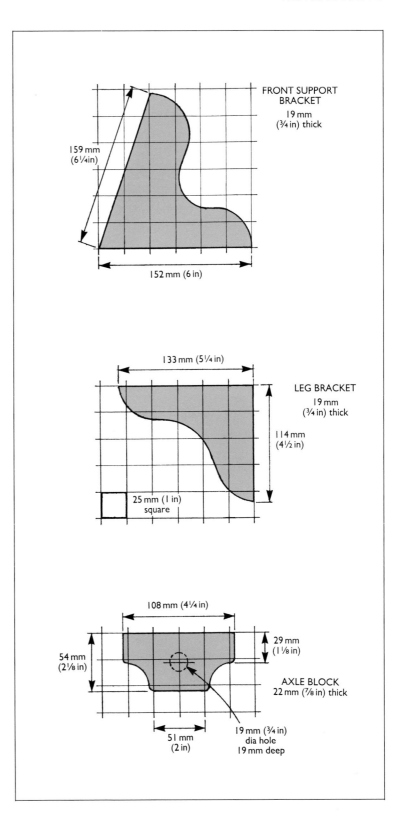

FRONT SUPPORT BRACKET
19 mm (¾ in) thick

159 mm (6¼ in)

152 mm (6 in)

LEG BRACKET
19 mm (¾ in) thick

133 mm (5¼ in)

114 mm (4½ in)

25 mm (1 in) square

108 mm (4¼ in)

54 mm (2⅛ in)

29 mm (1⅛ in)

AXLE BLOCK
22 mm (⅞ in) thick

51 mm (2 in)

19 mm (¾ in) dia hole 19 mm deep

## MONEY SAVER

If you buy sawn timber you can save a great deal of money. However it's quite a big job to plane it all smooth unless you have a hand-held electric planer. These machines are wonderful and will remove the roughness of the sawn cut, leaving a perfectly smooth piece of timber. If you do a lot of woodworking it's worth the investment.

## USEFUL TIP

If you are unfamiliar with electric saws then you couldn't do better than to start with a jigsaw. They will cut almost anything a circular saw can, and as they cut more slowly and have a reciprocating cutting action they are safer in use. A jigsaw will open the door to so many wonderful projects.

**8** With a coping saw now cut wooden brackets to support the front. After glasspapering smooth, the brackets are glued and screwed on to the handle-struts: the screws pass from the inside of the barrow front into the brackets. This method of securing the brackets and front on to the handle-struts works well, and makes for a very rigid fixing.

**9** The sides of the high-sided barrow also have to have an angle made on the bottom edge, corresponding to the angle along the bottom of the front piece. Plane the angle following the method outlined earlier (see Step 7).

Once the side pieces have been planed, put them in place against the front piece and it is at once evident that a further angle will have to be removed from each side at the front edge in order to get the three surfaces to fit flush to each other.

Planing the requisite angle on the front edges of the side pieces is not straightforward, for you are planing end grain. It is a good idea to re-sharpen the blade on your plane before starting. You will also need frequently to check your progress by placing the side pieces up against the front piece. Both sides have to be perfected before you proceed to the next step.

**10** When everything fits, glue the sides to the handle-struts and the front; use screws additionally to secure the sides to the front.

**11** The back of the barrow is treated in a similar manner. (I admit to having left it to last, and to having used a large piece of card to determine its size while making the prototype.) Again the task is to plane angles – and again you will need the sharpest of blades on your plane to tackle the end grain. A useful tip is to rub a lick of candle grease on the plane sole: it helps the task along considerably. Remember frequently to check on your progress by placing the back up against the sides – you can always plane more off, but you can't stick any back on!

**12** Once the back is in shape, glue and screw it in place. Drive the screws up from the underneath of the floor through the sides.

### THE WHEEL AND LEGS

**13** Now it is time to consider the wheel. A proper wooden wheel, complete with shaped spokes, is a beautiful piece of craftsmanship . . . which is not really necessary on a humble barrow. Use a compass to mark out a circle on a clean piece of wood (with no knots). As you remove the compass, mark clearly in pencil exactly where the centre is, and drill a hole there with a diameter the same as that of the dowel rod being used. Cut out the wheel carefully with a coping saw: it is not difficult, so don't be apprehensive. Alternatively, some electric jigsaws have an ingenious attachment that allows them to cut perfect circles of all sizes. But the coping saw is entirely adequate for the purpose.

**14** Now cut two battens to length to fit one on each side of the wheel at right-angles to each other. In the middle of each batten drill a hole large enough for the axle to pass through.

The axle is a ramin dowel rod. The best construction method is to fix the axle into the wheel – it should be a tight fit made solid with a spot of glue – and then fit the battens, threading them on to the wheel along the axle each side. Glue them on, aligning them so that one

Cutting out the Flower Barrow wheel using a compass cutting device.

strengthens the wood in the shortgrain direction. Use a couple of cramps to clamp the battens to the wheel while the glue cures. (Do not worry if either of the battens turns out to be a little long: edges can be trimmed later when the glue is dry and hard. And for now also leave cutting the axle to length each side of the wheel.)

**15** To trim the battens where they overlap the edge of the wheel, a spokeshave is the ideal tool. Chamfer off both the edges of the battens where necessary and around the edges of the wheel itself. Care is required. Finish off with glasspaper.

**16** Now cut the two axle blocks to size. In each, bore a hole to take the axle: the hole should be quite a degree larger than the axle diameter itself to allow for the angle at which the axle blocks are to be positioned. Cut the axle rod to length each side of the wheel. Rub candle wax into the axle block holes and on the ends of the axle. Then glue and screw the axle blocks on to the chassis, with the wheel in place between them.

**17** The legs are now marked up and cut to

**The wooden wheel for both barrows is strengthened on either side with battens. The dowel rod axle has liberal supplies of candle wax rubbed into it before assembly.**

length. The small rebate on the end is cut with a tenon saw. Carefully mark out in pencil the section to be removed, and use a cutting block to hold the leg firmly while you saw.

**18** Glue and screw the legs to the handle-struts. Then cut out angle blocks and glue them to the legs and the handle-struts: these serve a practical function but also add to the overall character of the design.

FINISHING OFF

It is essential that the wood is treated with a good wood preservative. But you may wish also to paint your barrow – a barrow can be quite a decorative item in its own right, after all. Use lead-free weather-resistant paint as bright as you like.

Painted or not, your barrow – the open or the high-sided type – will look good in your garden, rewarding you for your time and effort in making it.

# FOR CHILDREN AND NATURE LOVERS

THE GARDEN IS A FAVOURITE PLACE FOR CHILDREN AND

THEY'LL BE DELIGHTED WITH TWO OF THE PROJECTS IN THIS

SECTION – THE SANDBOX AND THE PLAY TOWER. ON THE

OTHER HAND, IF BIRDS ARE FREQUENT VISITORS, THEN THE

NESTBOXES AND BIRD TABLE WILL ENSURE YOU MANY

HOURS OF HAPPY BIRDWATCHING AND PROVIDE THEM WITH

A SAFE HAVEN.

# SANDBOX AND LID

CHILDREN TAKE GREAT DELIGHT IN PLAYING WITH SAND. AND NOT JUST CHILDREN – ON THE BEACH IT IS EVIDENT THAT MUMS, DADS, NANNIES AND GRANDPARENTS MAY BE JUST AS ENTHUSIASTIC CREATORS OF SANDCASTLES, ROAD SYSTEMS OR TEMPORARY PITS. HERE IS A SIMPLE WAY YOU CAN PROVIDE A SAFE PLACE FOR SAND FUN.

The trouble with having just a loose heap of sand in your garden is that not only does it tend to vanish into the earth beneath once rain starts to fall, but that local cats and dogs may discover it and put it to use in their own fashion so that it quickly becomes something of a health hazard. The answer is to keep your sand in a box with a lid.

This Project is one of the simplest, and may be an excellent one for a first-time amateur woodworker.

### STARTING OUT

1 Study the diagram and check that you have all the materials and tools listed below.

Then make a start by marking out and cutting to length the four sides of the box. Be sure to cut the wood perpendicularly: the edge must be square or the box won't join neatly at the corners.

Each corner has a block of wood enclosed in it, helping to make the joint but more importantly adding to the overall strength of the structure. It is possible to make the corners without a block, to screw one side to an end (to make a "butt joint"), but the disadvantage is that such a joint is not very strong, and in this case – especially in view of the weight of the sand – the corners really must be securely fastened.

For four corners, four blocks are required. Mark up and cut the blocks to length. When you have them, check that not only are the sides of each block at true right-angles with each other, but that the ends you have just sawn are also completely square. If they are not, you will experience difficulties later when you come to trying to square up the box as a unit.

### ASSEMBLING THE PARTS

2 To make the corners, start by gluing and screwing a block on to the inside edge at the end of one of the sides. You should make pilot holes for the screws, through the block and into the side, but be careful not to drill right through both pieces. For safety it would also be better to use a countersink bit at the top of each pilot hole so that the head of the screw will not protrude afterwards. Before driving in the screws, put a touch of waterproof glue on adjoining surfaces. Use zinc-plated Supascrews of some length and width – 50 mm long and 3 mm in diameter (2 in No. 8s) – for a really good job of fixing. When the block is on, and before the glue cures (sets), check again for squareness.

**This little Sandbox will give hours of pleasure to any youngster fortunate enough to find someone to make one for him or her. It is a good first-time project.**

The corners of the Sandbox are held together by the use of corner blocks. These blocks give tremendous rigidity to the box.

## SANDBOX AND LID CUTTING LIST

**Sides** 2 off 889 × 235 × 22 mm (35 × 9¼ × ⅞ in) timber

2 off 711 × 235 × 22 mm (28 × 9¼ × ⅞ in) timber

**Corner blocks** 4 off 235 × 44 × 44 mm (9¼ × 1¾ × 1¾ in) timber

**Base** 1 off 889 × 756 × 12 mm (35 × 29¾ × ½ in) plywood

**Spacer blocks** 8 off 127 × 64 × 22 mm (5 × 2½ × ⅞ in) timber

**Lid frame** 2 off 838 × 47 × 22 mm (33 × 1⅞ × ⅞ in) timber

2 off 620 × 47 × 22 mm (24⅜ × 1⅞ × ⅞ in) timber

**Lid** 1 off 914 × 774 mm (36 × 30½ in) clear corrugated plastic *or* plywood

## MATERIALS

Wood:

planks (for the sides)

posts (to make blocks for the corners and as feet underneath)

plywood *or* floorboarding (for the base)

plywood *or* corrugated plastic roofing material (for the lid)

battens (for the lid frame)

Zinc-plated Supascrews

Galvanized screws, cup-washers and caps (for a plastic lid)

Wood preservative

Paint

Silver sand

(see Cutting List)

Then fix the other three blocks to the other three sides, put the sides together, and glue and screw the whole framework together.

When the box sides have been assembled in this way, and again before the glue cures, check once more for squareness. The best method by which to do this at this stage is to use a long length of batten or dowel rod. Shape the batten or rod so that it has a pointed end, put the point into one corner of the box, and mark with a pencil along the batten or rod the exact position where it overlaps the box at the diagonally opposite corner. Now move the batten or rod around the box by one corner and see if the same measurement is precisely accurate from that corner to its diagonal opposite. If it is, as it should be, the box framework is square. If the measurement is out by any margin, exert a gentle pressure on one or other corner until the framework really is square. Then allow the glue to dry.

**3** The next task is to fit the base of the box on to the bottom of the sides. The wood for the base should be plywood or floorboarding. If you use plywood, it should be of "exterior grade" (and carry a W.P.B. marking). Use the completed box framework to mark up the required size of the base on the chosen plywood or boarding. Then cut it out.

Before attaching the base to the sides, first glue and screw small blocks of wood on the under surface at the corners, half-way down the longer edges, and symmetrically spaced each side of the centre (see the diagram). The blocks are to keep the sand box off the ground, allowing air to circulate underneath so as to prevent the rapid deterioration of the wood of the base.

Also before attaching the base to the sides, drill some holes in the base to allow for drainage just in case someone leaves the lid open during a rainstorm.

Then attach the base to the sides. Having drilled pilot holes, put a touch of glue on adjoining surfaces and drive screws through the base and into the widths of the box sides, and into the end grain of the corner blocks.

## THE LID

**4** A lid is essential. It can be made of exterior-grade plywood or – as I tend to prefer – corru-

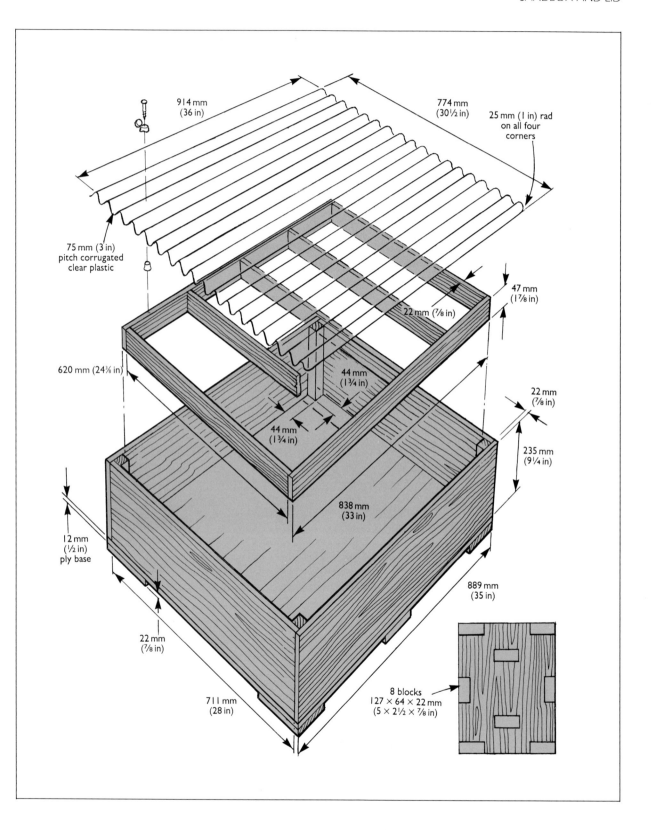

914 mm
(36 in)

774 mm
(30½ in)

25 mm (1 in) rad
on all four
corners

75 mm (3 in)
pitch corrugated
clear plastic

47 mm
(1⅞ in)

22 mm (⅞ in)

620 mm (24⅜ in)

44 mm
(1¾ in)

22 mm
(⅞ in)

44 mm
(1¾ in)

235 mm
(9¼ in)

838 mm
(33 in)

12 mm
(½ in)
ply base

889 mm
(35 in)

22 mm
(⅞ in)

711 mm
(28 in)

8 blocks
127 × 64 × 22 mm
(5 × 2½ × ⅞ in)

wood, it is nonetheless advisable to drill pilot holes in the battens to prevent the battens from splitting as the screws are driven in.

If you are making your lid with plywood, remember to leave a small overhang every side of the box, in order to allow rain to drain off well away from the sides. Glue and screw it on top of the frame. Round off the sharp edges of the plywood with glasspaper or a surform tool.

If you are using corrugated plastic instead, you will have to cut it to size using a fine-toothed saw (such as a tenon saw). Again leave an overlap for rain drainage, and cut the sharp corners off, using an old pair of scissors (or tin snips). If you leave a sharp corner, it is a certainty that sooner or later a child will snag a finger or face on it. The plastic is easy to shape when it is new – but after many years of exposure to sun and rain it may become brittle. Corrugated plastic is fixed to its frame by special galvanized screws, cup-washers and caps, generally available from where the plastic itself is obtained. Ideally, all screws should be driven in from the top of the corrugations: if they are fixed instead through the "valleys", the water that runs down the channels may find a way through. Use a sharp drill to make pilot holes in the plastic: forcing a screw directly through the plastic may shatter the sheet or create cracks. Place a plastic washer under each screw head, and drive the screw in until it exerts a gentle pressure on the top of the corrugation. Now, over the screw head, clip on the cap provided, so making a watertight joint.

A perspex lid prevents cats and dogs getting into the Sandbox. Special plastic cup-washers, galvanized screws and caps are available for fastening down the perspex to the wood framework.

gated plastic roofing material. I like the plastic roofing material because it is still possible to see the castles and other works of sand art inside the box with the lid closed over them. And I think it has a more friendly look.

But plastic or plywood, the lid will need a framework. The frame is a simple square made from wooden battens cut accurately to length and then glued and screwed together. Although the twin threads of zinc-plated Supascrews are excellent in gripping even in the end grain of

### FINISHING OFF

Finish off the sand box by giving it three thorough coats of a good wood preservative, and then paint it a nice, bright colour using non-toxic, weatherproof paint.

When the inside is completely dry, it is time to fill the box with sand. The best type of sand to use is silver sand, available in plastic sacks of various sizes from builders' merchants and some DIY stores. Other types of sand may stain hands and clothes.

# PLAY TOWER

CHILDREN LOVE CLIMBING. MOST ALSO HAVE WONDERFUL IMAGINATIONS – AND THIS TOWER SHOULD GIVE THEM TREMENDOUS SCOPE FOR ACTION AND FUN. AT THE SAME TIME, I HAVE DESIGNED IT VERY SPECIFICALLY BOTH FOR SAFETY AND FOR STRENGTH AND STABILITY, YET IT IS NOT DIFFICULT TO CONSTRUCT, OR TO HANDLE WHEN PUT TOGETHER.

**W**hen you make anything for children to play in or on, several factors have to be kept constantly in mind. Safety is one – perhaps the most important – and includes not only the materials and design of the structure but also its overall stability when youngsters swarm all over it. Strength and longevity have also to be considered, and in relation to the cost.

In a larger garden containing adventure playthings of this kind, there has also to be a certain amount of teaching that parents, guardians and grandparents must do before their charges are let loose. There should be few restrictions placed on a climbing tower of this kind – but some basic safety rules should be made quite clear before activity on it begins.

As for the construction, do not let its completed size daunt you: look at the whole in its separate parts and you will see that it is not too heavy or difficult to handle. Although the legs are simply bolted together – so minimizing weight and cutting cost – and although the safety-cage at the top is constructed simply of battens, the whole structure is fixed together using coach-screws. The coach-screw has a squared head and a large, coarse thread, and when fitted with a large washer under the head can exert tremendous clamping pressure on

two adjoining struts. The ladder is likewise easily made, using dowel rods of large diameter for the rungs.

## STARTING OUT

**1** First study the diagrams, and make sure that you have everything you need and that you understand what has to be done.

Start by constructing the legs of the tower. Each leg is made of four pieces of wood: at top and bottom are two solid chunks of post 10 × 10 cm (4 × 4 in) in cross-section, connected by two planks of wood screwed in on opposite sides. Cut to length all the solid chunks, or stubs, that go between the planks, noting that the vertical length is different for top and bottom stubs (see Cutting List).

With a pencil, mark on the sides of the planks where the coach-screws are to go. Then drill fairly large pilot holes in all the planks: eight for each leg (two horizontally parallel at top and bottom of each plank). The hole can actually be as large as the coach-screw shank, for the screw is to go through the hole into a stub, and it is in the stub that the screw must be tight.

When the pilot holes in the planks have been drilled, take two planks and position a top and a bottom stub at either end between them. Fix planks and stubs temporarily together with

*Above:* A typical bottom leg; note the centre stub and planks coach-bolted to it. Steel sockets are used in all four corners.
*Right:* This Play Tower will give youngsters a wonderful sense of adventure.

holes. All you need to bear in mind at this point, though, is that not all of the screws are in place permanently, and that for now the initial fixing of the legs together is essential for construction purposes.

### ASSEMBLING THE PARTS

**2** The legs are now to be joined together with struts. Each leg has two sides on which the central stub is still visible between planks, and two sides on which planks cover the stub by a margin. The four struts that join the legs will therefore comprise two which attach to planks covering a stub, and two which can be screwed direct into the stub provided that the outer overhang margin is cut away first.

To make one of the two sides that attach flat against the outside plank of the legs, position the two legs at the right distance apart, flat on the ground, with the heads of the coach-screws prominent. Then place the joining strut between them, over the screw heads, and give the strut a sharp tap with a fairly hefty hammer – enough at least to make a clear imprint of the screw heads on the strut. You can now use those imprints as a guide to where pilot holes can be drilled. Remove the coach-screws that created the imprint; place the new strut in position, hole for hole; and screw the coach-screws back in tight. You may have to ask two helpers to keep things steady for you as you do this.

Make the other similar side in exactly the same way.

**3** To make one of the two sides that attach directly to the central stub of the legs, measure the width of the strut that is going to join the two legs, and with a pencil mark that width on the outer overhang of the plank at the top of the leg. Now with a saw and chisel, remove the marked section of plank on the leg, making it possible for the strut joining the legs together to be positioned flush against the central stub of the leg, and thus to be screwed directly into the stub. This may sound rather difficult, but if you look at the photographs of a typical leg section, and

clamps, and from each side in turn drill through the existing pilot holes a much smaller pilot hole in the stubs for the coach-screw to go into. Starting with one side, put in the screws at top and bottom. Zinc-plated screws (and washers) are best but are not always available, so you may have to resort to steel coach-screws and paint them well at the finish. At first put the screws in only lightly, and when all four are in position – and when the position and squareness also of the receiving stub has been checked – tighten them up. Then turn over to the other side and complete the leg in similar fashion.

Repeat the operation with the remaining three legs.

The four legs are then complete. But at the very next stage some of the coach-screws you have just screwed in and tightened up will have to come out again. This is because the struts that are to join the legs together will be fastened on by using some of the same screws in the same

study the diagram, you will quickly see how it is supposed to go together. In a sense this is engineering in wood – there is little finesse: this construction is all large pieces of wood that are simply screwed together.

**4** At the top of the tower framework, two extra struts are now fitted to the inside edges of the legs in order to give the floor planks extra

One top corner of the tower. Note the four cross-timbers bolted to the legs, to give added strength to the floor.

support – support particularly necessary when a whole group of children is on board.

Again position each strut against the coach-screw heads of the two legs, and tap with a hammer to get the imprints that then act as

## PLAY TOWER CUTTING LIST

**Tower leg stubs** 8 off 610 × 98 × 98 mm (24 × 3⅞ × 3⅞ in) timber

**Leg verticals** 8 off 1372 × 124 × 22 mm (54 × 4⅞ × ⅞ in) timber

**Front/rear struts** 4 off 1372 × 124 × 22 mm (54 × 4⅞ × ⅞ in) timber

**Side cross-struts** 6 off 1372 × 124 × 22 mm (54 × 4⅞ × ⅞ in) timber

**Platform floor** 2 off 895 × 124 × 22 mm (35¼ × 4⅞ × ⅞ in) timber

5 off 1372 × 149 × 22 mm (54 × 5⅞ × ⅞ in) timber

**Safety cage** 2 off 1245 × 57 × 22 mm (49 × 2¼ × ⅞ in) timber

5 off 914 × 47 × 47 mm (36 × 1⅞ × 1⅞ in) timber

5 off 1187 × 57 × 22 mm (46¾ × 2¼ × ⅞ in) timber

10 off 1092 × 57 × 22 mm (43 × 2¼ × ⅞ in) timber

3 off 413 × 57 × 22 mm (16¼ × 2¼ × ⅞ in) timber

3 off 660 × 57 × 22 mm (26 × 2¼ × ⅞ in) timber

**Ladder verticals** 2 off 2134 × 73 × 22 mm (84 × 2⅞ × ⅞ in) timber

**Ladder rungs** 8 off 25 mm diam. × 381 mm length (1 in diam. × 15 in length) dowel

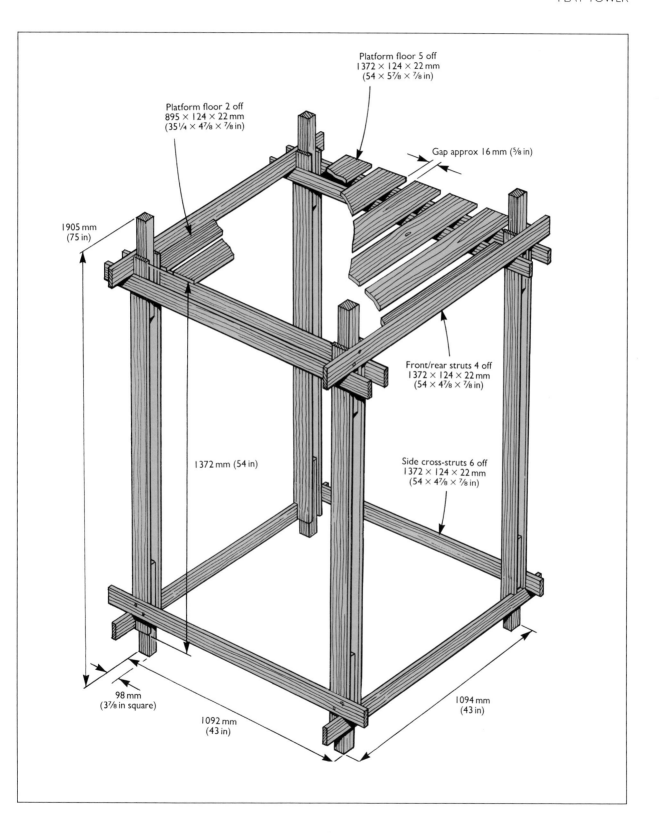

Platform floor 5 off
1372 × 124 × 22 mm
(54 × 5⁷⁄₈ × ⁷⁄₈ in)

Platform floor 2 off
895 × 124 × 22 mm
(35¼ × 4⁷⁄₈ × ⁷⁄₈ in)

Gap approx 16 mm (⁵⁄₈ in)

1905 mm
(75 in)

Front/rear struts 4 off
1372 × 124 × 22 mm
(54 × 4⁷⁄₈ × ⁷⁄₈ in)

1372 mm (54 in)

Side cross-struts 6 off
1372 × 124 × 22 mm
(54 × 4⁷⁄₈ × ⁷⁄₈ in)

98 mm
(3⁷⁄₈ in square)

1092 mm
(43 in)

1094 mm
(43 in)

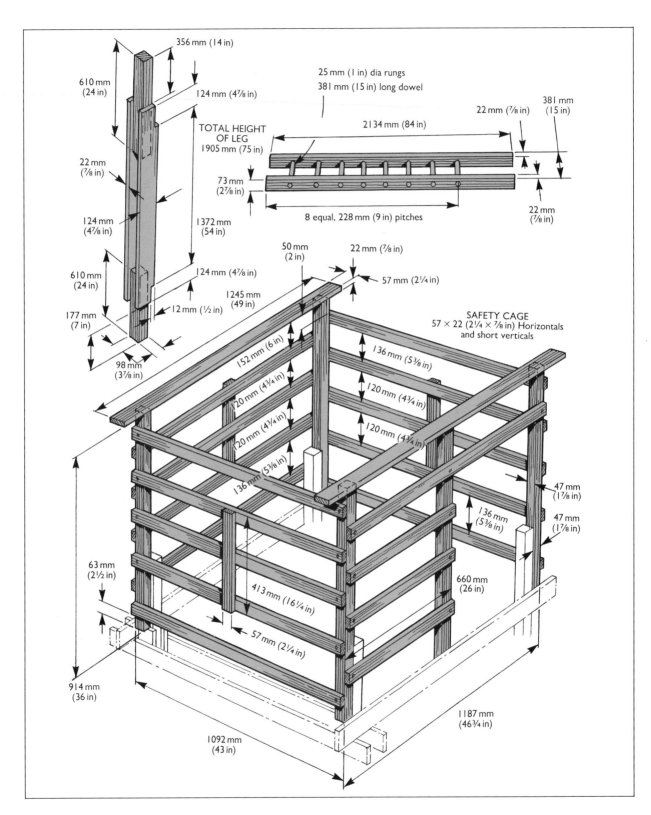

356 mm (14 in)

610 mm
(24 in)

124 mm (4⅞ in)

25 mm (1 in) dia rungs
381 mm (15 in) long dowel

22 mm (⅞ in)

381 mm
(15 in)

2134 mm (84 in)

TOTAL HEIGHT
OF LEG
1905 mm (75 in)

22 mm
(⅞ in)

73 mm
(2⅞ in)

124 mm
(4⅞ in)

1372 mm
(54 in)

8 equal, 228 mm (9 in) pitches

22 mm
(⅞ in)

610 mm
(24 in)

124 mm (4⅞ in)

50 mm
(2 in)

22 mm (⅞ in)

57 mm (2¼ in)

12 mm (½ in)

1245 mm
(49 in)

SAFETY CAGE
57 × 22 (2¼ × ⅞ in) Horizontals
and short verticals

177 mm
(7 in)

98 mm
(3⅞ in)

152 mm (6 in)

136 mm (5⅜ in)

120 mm (4¾ in)

120 mm (4¾ in)

120 mm (4¾ in)

136 mm (5⅜ in)

47 mm
(1⅞ in)

136 mm
(5⅜ in)

47 mm
(1⅞ in)

63 mm
(2½ in)

413 mm (16¼ in)

57 mm (2¼ in)

660 mm
(26 in)

914 mm
(36 in)

1187 mm
(46¾ in)

1092 mm
(43 in)

locators for pilot holes. Drill the holes; remove the coach-screws; fit the strut; replace the coach-screws, and tighten up.

## THE CAGE

**5** The "cage" on top of the tower legs is very important. A protective rail runs all around the top, even over the gap that represents the way in, or entry port, and is intended to prevent children who are running around in the tower from falling out.

The cage is made from horizontal battens coach-screwed to upright posts at the four corners, and a fifth upright that forms the doorpost for the entry port. It would be easy to screw the four corner posts directly on to the tower legs, and then to screw the battens to the posts. But for painting and for maintenance thereafter, it is useful to be able to remove the whole cage easily as a unit – to make it secure while in position, but detachable when required. (Nothing is more difficult than struggling above your head to remove or refit one part of an integrated structure.) This detachability can be achieved by fitting small strips of batten beneath each of the four upright posts: a thickness of some 3 mm (⅛ in) should be ideal. Resting on these corner pads, the cage can be speedily removed and as quickly refitted, and the tiny extra width will also allow for thickness of paint on the cage.

In fitting the horizontal battens of the cage to the corner-posts, it is important to drill pilot holes for the coach-screws, for the battens are considerably lighter in section than the posts, and without pilot holes the screws may split the battens – an ugly sight.

**6** The rail at the top is also secured by screws to the corner-posts. These should be fairly long screws – 60 mm (2½ in) – of some width – 4 mm (⅙ in, No. 10) – in order to get a solid fixing.

**7** The cage is fixed to the tower framework beneath by coach-screws. Two coach-screws per post are quite sufficient. Make sure that a

The safety cage on the top of the Play Tower is screwed together. This cage is then further screwed to the legs of the tower. The whole structure is immensely rigid.

washer is fitted beneath the heads of all the screws, or the screw heads may damage the wood when tightened, and the overall grip of the joint will be reduced.

## THE LADDER

**8** The ladder is easier to construct than you may think. But you must be sure to have obtained dowel rod of at least 24 mm (1 in) diameter: such dowel rods often come in 1.9 m (6 ft) lengths.

Select two lengths of wood to make the ladder sides. It is *vital* not only that these two lengths are completely free of knots but that the wood has an even, straight grain. The reason for being so particular is simply one of strength: a knot represents an inherent weakness in the wood, an irregular grain may correspond to the same thing.

Temporarily fasten together both lengths with tape, clearly marking on them with a pencil which way round they are. Taking the dimen-

> **SAFETY TIP**
> Those jobs that take a little more time are often the most rewarding. However the key to success with any woodworking project is to have sharp tools. Accidents will happen if you have to struggle and strain with a chisel, for example, but if it's properly sharpened then it will slice easily through the wood. Buy yourself a new oil stone to make the sharpening process easier, and a jug for holding chisels.

> **TOWER TESTERS**
> When installed in a children's playground this playtower instantly had the attention of five youngsters all running and jumping around the top platform.

sions from the diagram, use the pencil to mark out the centres of the rungs along the top length. Then drill the holes for the rungs through both lengths at once. For this, the ideal tool is an electric drill with a stand: the stand ensures that a hole drilled is vertical both in terms of the length of the wood and in relation to its width. If you have no drill stand, some hire shops rent them – but it is possible in practice to do without. For those who are not confident, an alternative method is to ask a helper to keep a close eye on one dimension while you yourself maintain a careful watch on the other, as you drill. A hole drilled at the wrong angle, though, will make final assembly difficult.

**9** Now cut the rungs to length from the dowel. It is important that they are all of identical length because it is the length of the dowel rungs that determines the overall width of the ladder. A way to ensure this is first to make yourself a small measuring-stick against which to compare each rung as you complete it.

When all the rungs are cut to length, create a chamfer (smooth the sharp edge off) around each end of each rung using glasspaper wrapped around a wooden block.

**10** Unfasten the ladder sides from their tape, and place one side down on a flat surface. Run a little waterproof glue around the holes, and start inserting the rungs one by one on the inner side of the ladder length (as marked when the sides were taped together). If they are a tight fit, tap them in with a hammer over a block of wood: do *not* let the hammer itself touch the dowel rungs or you may spoil the chamfer, distort the end of the rung, and so make it impossible to get the rung in at all. Each rung should eventually go through the ladder length until the end of the rung is flush with the outside edge.

You will end up with one side of the ladder and all the rungs sticking out at right-angles from it. Now comes the time to fit on the other ladder side . . . which is slightly more difficult. Run a little glue around the holes of the second side, and position it against the rungs (making sure the ladder side is the correct way round, as marked when they were taped together). Gently fit the rungs into the holes: one or two may need a little coaxing, not to say coercion. Then use the hammer over the wooden block again to tap on the second side. If you encounter a solid resistance, then one of the rungs is not in its hole: check, and reinsert it if necessary. Work along the entire length of the ladder with the block and hammer, keeping the side as even as possible.

As the dowel rungs approach becoming flush with the outer edge of the ladder, hammering in this way may no longer be so effective as the resistance increases because of the heightened friction. If you have a large enough vice, the best method now is to put the ladder in the vice and squeeze the sides together. But without a vice, you will have to use a heavy hammer (over the wooden block) and hit even harder. Whatever you do, do not stop to have a cup of tea – you have glued the holes, remember – or you will never get the ladder together!

The dowel rungs flush at both sides, the ladder is complete.

## FINISHING OFF

The ladder fits neatly into the cage, and there is room for you to coach-screw it to the side of the tower leg. It is advisable to fix the ladder to the leg in this way: you can be sure if you don't that there will come a time when the ladder slips and someone will be hurt.

It only remains for you to screw the floor in place, and the tower is finished. The timber used for the floor is well supported on the four timbers that run beneath. Space the floor planks equidistant across the top bearers, placing the two shorter lengths one on either side between the uprights as shown in the diagram. Use zinc-plated screws to attach the floor planks to the wood beneath. Countersink the holes to ensure that no screw heads will protrude.

After coating the entire construction with a good wood preservative, paint it in any colour or pattern you choose. Use paint that is non-toxic but weather-resistant.

The whole tower must then be securely fixed in the ground. For this I strongly recommend the use of steel spiked sockets into which the legs can be inserted. Some of the sockets now commercially available (under different names in different countries) have barbs on their inner surfaces, so that when the posts are inserted into them they are retained there. Some sockets also have perforated holes in the sides through which securing screws may additionally be inserted. Such sockets keep wooden legs out of the wet at ground level and relieve already hard-pressed tower-builders of any need to dig deep holes. Instead, they are readily driven into the ground using a sledge-hammer. Mind your fingers. And before you actually start driving spikes into the ground,

**Any Play Tower has to be built with the assumption that children will swarm all over it. The ladder is firmly coach-bolted to the leg and to the frame. Ideally the end of the ladder should be sunk into the ground.**

check there are no water-pipes, electricity cables or other dangers in the vicinity.

Once the sockets have been driven into the ground, you will need assistance to lift your tower construction into them. You may need even to cut small "keyways" into the sides of the legs to enable the legs to be driven firmly past the barbs on the sockets down to the full depth of the sockets. The keyways will then allow the barbs to get a firm grip.

Do not place paving stones or concrete any-where near the tower. Bark chippings as a play area surface is a good idea and creates a soft landing for children who leap off ladders. For further advice, consult your local Children's Safety Officer.

---

### USEFUL TIP

Assembling and lifting this tower is a job for a number of people. Due to the weight of the tower, at least four people are needed to get it into the steel sockets.

# NESTBOXES

IN SO MANY GARDENS AND PARKS THERE IS A PLENTIFUL FOOD
SUPPLY FOR SMALL BIRDS BUT NOWHERE FOR THEM TO NEST –
NOWHERE, PERHAPS, UNTIL YOU HAVE READ THIS CHAPTER
AND RUSH IMMEDIATELY TO YOUR WOODWORK BENCH
INSPIRED TO BUILD A COUPLE OF BOXES!

## TOOLS YOU WILL NEED

A SAW

A PENCIL

A RULE OR MEASURE

A DRILL
bit for screws
flat bits (for entrance holes
of more than one size)

A PLANE *or*
SURFORM TOOL

A HAMMER

WATERPROOF GLUE

A CLAMP

A hole 27–28 mm (1 1/16 in) in diameter will tempt a coal, marsh or blue tit; a 30 mm (1 1/8 in) diameter hole for great tit; and a 32 mm (1 1/4 in) diameter hole for nuthatches and tree sparrows.

**B**irds are some of the very best friends a garden can have: they eat scaly insects, aphids, caterpillars, and other unwelcome horticultural guests. Watching birds nesting in boxes you have provided is extremely rewarding – but your real reward is the sight of their colour and movement and the sound of their song in summer.

The boxes themselves can be made very easily, and a sharp saw, hammer, drill, and screws are all you need. Each nestbox must be a minimum of 100 mm (4 in) square. The bottom of the entrance hole must be at least 125 mm (5 in) from the floor: if it is less, there is the dire possibility that fledgling birds may be scooped out by a cat's paw.

In the wild, each type of bird makes an entrance hole to its nest of a size particular to its own species, so the diameter of the hole you bore in the nestbox you make will be a critical factor in determining the type of bird you get as a summertime lodger.

The inside surfaces of the box should be rough, so if you buy planed or smooth wood you will need to roughen it up, especially the front inner surface, to allow the little birds some toeholds. You could stick pieces of old glasspaper to the interior walls. Do not fit a perch on the front – it might encourage sparrows to take an unhealthy interest in the

smaller birds that nest inside, and it also gives other predators a "step-up" into the box.

But if you provide a nestbox, you must remember to clean out the box every year once the summer is truly over. (In some countries, any unhatched eggs still inside may legally be removed only during autumn and winter months.) The box should be taken down from its site and the inside thoroughly sterilized with boiling water, or mites and ticks that infest birds will live on in the old nesting material and plague the new young of the following season. Do not use disinfectant. Make sure it is properly dried afterwards, and check that the drain hole at the bottom of the box is not blocked – pick it through with a piece of wire.

Nestboxes may be used by birds as roosting places in winter, so you are providing potential shelter for them throughout the year.

## STARTING OUT

**1** First, study the drawing. It is easier to mark the whole thing out on a length of plank. If you use this method, however, you must remember that the saw cut between each piece may be thicker in reality than the pencil line that marks it out. As with any job, if you don't have the right

**A Nestbox gives the maker a sense of satisfaction as the "house" becomes occupied.**

## MATERIALS

A plank

Screws

Strip of felt, roofing felt, *or*
  rubber

Felt-nails

Hook and eye

Wood preservative

Wire *or* nylon cord

(Old pieces of glasspaper)

(see Cutting List)

tools the whole operation becomes a chore, not a pleasure: a really sharp handsaw is an absolute prerequisite for this job. With the saw, cut out the components of the structure.

**2** The angled tops of the side pieces may need a little trimming with a wood plane. To make sure that they remain parallel it is best to clamp them together and plane them as a pair. If the box is to be attached to a tree, drill holes in the top and bottom of the back piece, large enough to take screws or nails. (String should not be used to attach the box to the tree: it rots, and may give way when a family of young birds is in the box.)

A close-fitting lid with a hinge is necessary to facilitate cleaning the box in the autumn.

## NESTBOX CUTTING LIST

**Back** 1 off 406 × 152 × 22 mm (16 × 6 × ⅞ in) timber

**Sides** 2 off 254 × 152 × 22 mm (10 × 6 × ⅞ in) timber

**Front** 1 off 203 × 152 × 22 mm (8 × 6 × ⅞ in) timber

**Base** 1 off 184 × 152 × 22 mm (7¼ × 6 × ⅞ in) timber

**Lid** 1 off 203 × 152 × 22 mm (8 × 6 × ⅞ in) timber

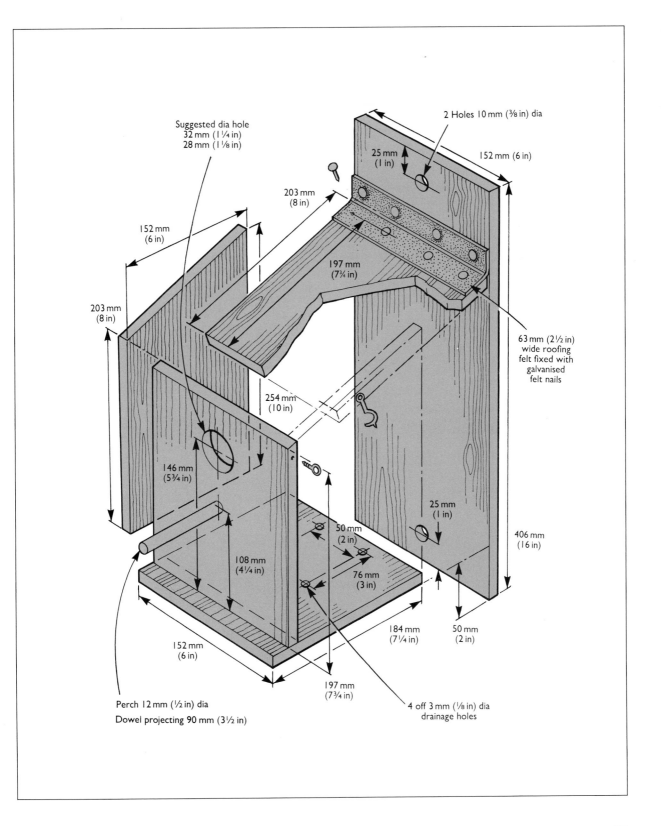

2 Holes 10 mm (³⁄₈ in) dia

152 mm (6 in)

25 mm
(1 in)

Suggested dia hole
32 mm (1¼ in)
28 mm (1⅛ in)

203 mm
(8 in)

152 mm
(6 in)

197 mm
(7¾ in)

203 mm
(8 in)

63 mm (2½ in)
wide roofing
felt fixed with
galvanised
felt nails

254 mm
(10 in)

146 mm
(5¾ in)

25 mm
(1 in)

406 mm
(16 in)

108 mm
(4¼ in)

50 mm
(2 in)

76 mm
(3 in)

152 mm
(6 in)

184 mm
(7¼ in)

50 mm
(2 in)

197 mm
(7¾ in)

Perch 12 mm (½ in) dia
Dowel projecting 90 mm (3½ in)

4 off 3 mm (⅛ in) dia
drainage holes

A piece of roofing felt acts as both a hinge and a weather strip. The roofing felt tacked to the back will prevent water getting into the box. Be generous with the felt nails.

## ASSEMBLING THE PARTS

**3** The side pieces should be screwed to the back. Drill pilot holes through the back, then both gluing and screwing the sides to it. Screw the base in place. Now position the front and lid against the box and you will find that the sloping angle of the sides will prevent the lid from closing down flush. Mark with a pencil on the front piece how far down the sides come, due to the angle of the slope, and use a wood plane or surform plane to remove the excess wood. Every now and then place the front up against the sides again to check progress as you work.

**4** Before you actually fit on the front, however, you must first bore the entrance hole through it, at the size selected. Drills can be expensive, but there is a wood-boring bit specially developed for electric drills: the flat bit. These are comparatively inexpensive and are available in a whole range of sizes. The wood to be drilled must be firmly clamped in a vice *before* you attempt to drill the hole. The flat bit has a long spike at its tip: the best method is to drill into the wood until the spike appears through on the other side. Stop the drill, turn the wood over, insert the flat bit spike into the hole, and – after having resecured the wood – complete the hole. This method prevents the hole from being ragged.

Now glue and screw the front in place.

**5** Once more place the lid on top of the nestbox to check fit. Note how the front edge of the lid only makes contact with the front along its under edge. How much neater altogether it would be if it fitted flush . . . Again mark in pencil the angle of wood to be removed and, using a plane or surform tool, gently remove it. This really does make for a very tidy and neat fitting of the lid.

Use a hook and eye to fasten the lid securely. (Do not screw the lid down.)

**6** Now drill a couple of small holes in the base, to provide drainage just in case water gets in.

## FINISHING OFF

The lid should be attached to the back by a strip of felt or of rubber (such as a piece of cycle innertube): a strip of roofing felt is ideal. Attach the felt to the lid first, using felt-nails, and then to the back of the box. Be generous with the felt-nails and hammer them in firmly along the back edge, for this is a place where water could otherwise leak into the box.

All of the exterior of the box must be treated with a wood preservative. Do not treat the inside or the entrance hole.

When you get into the swing of boxmaking it is surprising just how many wood offcuts can be used up for this job.

# OWL NESTBOX

THERE IS SOMETHING VERY SPECIAL ABOUT OWLS. THEIR SILENT FLIGHT, THEIR HUGE, STARRY, YELLOW EYES AND FROWNING EXPRESSION, AND THEIR LONG-DRAWN-OUT CRY IN THE DUSK AND DARKNESS ALL GIVE OWLS SOMETHING OF A DISTINCTIVE CHARACTER.

W hen the time of year comes round once again for an owl to begin to obey the nesting instinct, it does not go looking for nest material but instead seeks ready-made natural nesting sites. Any of the smaller types of owl, because of its size, is able to make use of a far greater number of holes and crevices than its larger relatives, and will certainly use a well-made box if it seems to its liking.

A box for a little owl differs from other nestboxes in that it has a much larger hole at the front and a long, dark chamber inside. Owls like a good perch, so it is essential to provide a suitably solid one inside. I like to think that a shelter over the entrance is an almost irresistible further inducement to any self-respecting owl to take up residence in the box.

## STARTING OUT

1  First, cut the wood components to length and shape. Special care is required in cutting the front and back pieces. In fact, the large hole in the front piece presents the most difficult element of all in constructing this box. The diameter of the hole should be 70 mm (2¾ in), and

Although this box is intended for the little owl, it is still a fairly big construction and requires careful siting in a tree. Once it is in the tree make sure you fix it securely. This one has an inspection hatch in the roof and a good solid perch inside.

## TOOLS YOU WILL NEED

A SAW

A PENCIL

A RULE OR MEASURE

A SCREWDRIVER

A MEANS OF CUTTING A CIRCULAR HOLE
(a coping saw *or* a jigsaw *or* tank cutters)

A DRILL

WATERPROOF GLUE

Cutting the large diameter hole for the Owl Nestbox. Note the tank cutter – this is rather like a pastry cutter. A powerful drill is needed to drive this attachment.

## OWL NESTBOX CUTTING LIST

**Front and back** 2 off 203 × 203 × 22 mm (8 × 8 × ⅞ in) timber

**Roof** 2 off 711 × 225 × 22 mm (28 × 8 ⅞ × ⅞ in) timber

**Sides** 2 off 559 × 203 × 22 mm (22 × 8 × ⅞ in) timber

**Battens** 2 off 711 × 32 × 32 mm (28 × 1¼ × 1¼ in) timber

**Perch** 1 off 12 mm diam. × 89 mm length (½ in diam. × 3½ in length) dowel

## MATERIALS

Wood:

  boards

  battens

Zinc-plated Supascrews

Hinge

2 small dowel rods

Catch, *or* hook and eye

Wire

(Screw eyes)

(see Cutting List)

## USEFUL TIP

Drilling large holes can spoil expensive drill bits. However, for only a few pounds a set of tank hole cutters can be bought. These are available in a variety of sizes and they all fit into one holder.

it can be cut out in any of several ways. Plumbers use a set of circular cutters called tank cutters which, when mounted in a holder, fit into an ordinary electric drill. But if you cannot get hold of such things, an alternative is to use a jigsaw.

### ASSEMBLING THE PARTS

**2** It is now time to screw the sides on to the front and back pieces. Use both screws and glue: it helps to waterproof the joints. The roof pieces will overhang to create the "porch" covering the entrance hole.

**3** To strengthen the whole construction, glue battens along the top and bottom edges of the walls. The top batten additionally prevents water from seeping in, and the bottom batten provides the ideal perch for the owl. A small dowel rod beneath the entrance hole inside and out makes ingress and egress even easier for the owl – the height of sybaritic luxury, surely.

**4** To make an inspection hatch in the roof – essential for removing nest debris and for cleaning out the box generally – it is vital to provide a framework for it inside the box con-

struction. Without a framework inside, it is likely that a door will allow rainwater to leak through at the edges. The frame is made up of one batten that runs the full length of the roof at the width of the door, another batten of the same cross-sectional dimensions glued between the first batten and the side, and the battens at the top edge along the walls. All four edges of the door are thus shielded from inside by a batten. The door is then cut out of the roof, and attached at one edge by a hinge.

**5** The inspection hatch should normally be kept closed by a trustworthy catch, a hook and eye, or a small bolt.

### FINISHING OFF

Finally, some more holes must be drilled. Drill a small number in the base, to allow any water that does get in to drain out again. Drill some more in the top and bottom battens in order to wire the entire box on to a tree – the wire will have to be strong, for the box is no lightweight construction. Alternatively, fix large screw eyes to both top and bottom: these make excellent anchorage points for fixing.

Fix the box to a tree above the head height of any animals that might graze beneath it. Owls particularly like trees or stumps at the edges of fields or open land.

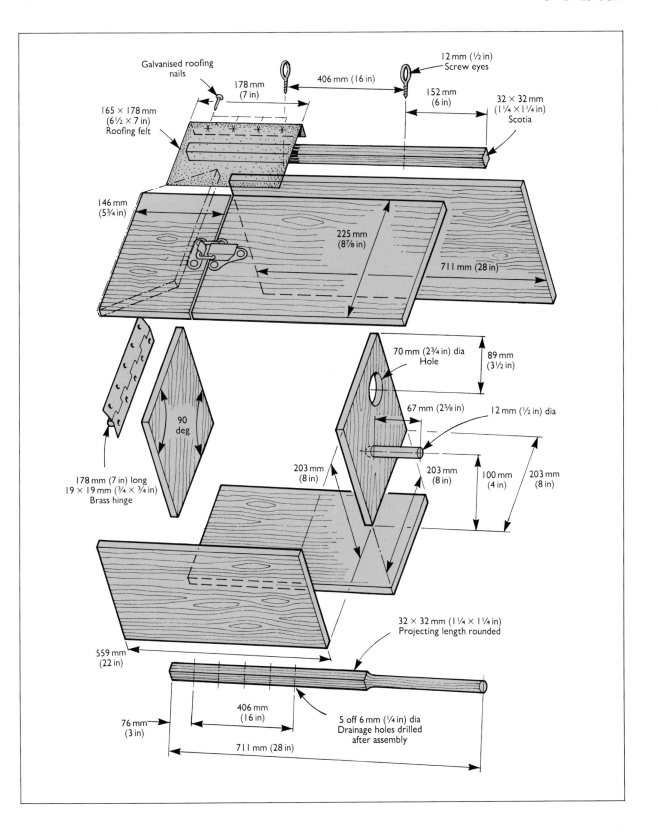

Galvanised roofing nails

178 mm (7 in)

12 mm (½ in) Screw eyes

406 mm (16 in)

165 × 178 mm (6½ × 7 in) Roofing felt

152 mm (6 in)

32 × 32 mm (1¼ × 1¼ in) Scotia

146 mm (5¾ in)

225 mm (8⅞ in)

711 mm (28 in)

70 mm (2¾ in) dia Hole

89 mm (3½ in)

67 mm (2⅝ in)

12 mm (½ in) dia

90 deg

178 mm (7 in) long 19 × 19 mm (¾ × ¾ in) Brass hinge

203 mm (8 in)

203 mm (8 in)

100 mm (4 in)

203 mm (8 in)

32 × 32 mm (1¼ × 1¼ in) Projecting length rounded

559 mm (22 in)

406 mm (16 in)

76 mm (3 in)

711 mm (28 in)

5 off 6 mm (¼ in) dia Drainage holes drilled after assembly

127

# BIRD TABLE

THERE CAN BE FEW GREATER PLEASURES THAN WATCHING
GARDEN BIRDS FEEDING AT A BIRD TABLE DURING THE DARKER,
COLDER MONTHS OF THE YEAR. FOR THE EFFORT AND TIME IT
TAKES TO CONSTRUCT A TABLE YOU WILL BE REPAID MANY
TIMES OVER IN THE COLOUR, MOVEMENT, AND VARIETY OF
BIRDS THAT COME TO TAKE ADVANTAGE OF YOUR
HANDIWORK AND OF THE FOOD YOU PROVIDE UPON IT.

## TOOLS YOU WILL NEED

A SAW
A PENCIL
A RULE OR MEASURE
A SCREWDRIVER
A DRILL
bit for screws
countersink bit
A PLANE
WATERPROOF GLUE
A CLAMP
A PUTTY-KNIFE *or*
A PLASTIC SPATULA

The table itself is best positioned on top of a post or stake, and well away from any overhanging ledges or branches from which marauding cats or squirrels might attempt to launch an airborne attack. Immediately beneath it, transfixed on the post, an inverted biscuit tin or tray with a deep edge is a useful addition to prevent those same bandits from raiding the table.

It is not essential for the table to be roofed, but in my view it is worth the extra effort it takes. A heavy fall of snow can cover the food faster than the birds can eat it, and they probably won't find it if they don't see it. A roof also provides extra places from which to hang bags of nuts.

### STARTING OUT

**1** First study the drawing. Then make a start with the post and the legs. The longer the legs are, the more potentially stable the table will be. Nonetheless, if your table is to have a roof it will be essential to use wooden or metal staples (hoops) to pin the legs to the ground surface, or any strong, gusting wind may blow the entire structure over. Alternatively, a stainless steel socket with a spiked tip – available in many sizes

Fixing the legs to the bottom of the Bird Table post. The legs for the Letterbox (see page 47) are fixed in the same way.

to fit posts of different dimensions – will ensure the stability of the table.

Following the plan, then, cut the four legs to shape. (It is not essential to shape the ends, but it does look better.) In my construction method I have avoided the more complicated traditional

This Bird Table should give years of service and is designed to allow birds to feed throughout the winter, when snow and heavy rain are falling.

128

Gluing and screwing the battens to the top of the Bird Table post.

## MATERIALS

A wooden post

Timber struts (for legs)

Nordic whitewood board
(for table)

Zinc-plated Supascrews

Tongued-and-grooved
boarding

Wood for battens

Roofing felt (light weight)

Fascia strips

Bitumastic compound

Wood preservative

Felt-nails

(Wooden or metal staples/
hoops for pinning table
down to earth, or steel
socket with spiked tip
anchoring post to the
ground)

(Screw eyes)

(see Cutting List)

## BIRD TABLE CUTTING LIST

**Post** I off 1524 × 73 × 73 mm (60 × 2⅞ ×
2⅞ in) timber

**Legs** 4 off 660 × 73 × 22 mm (26 × 2⅞ × ⅞ in)
timber

**Bearers** 2 off 508 × 73 × 22 mm (20 × 2⅞ ×
⅞ in) timber

**Table top** I off 508 × 267 × 16 mm (20 × 10½
× ⅝ in) timber

**Side battens** 2 off 438 × 51 × 22 mm (17¼ ×
2 × ⅞ in) timber

**End battens** 2 off 267 × 51 × 22mm (10½ × 2
× ⅞ in) timber

**Roof supports** 2 off 368 × 64 × 22 mm (14½
× 2½ × ⅞ in) timber

**Roof ends** 2 off 406 × 152 × 22 mm (16 × 6 ×
⅞ in) timber

**Roof** make from 4250 × 114 × 16 mm (165 ×
4½ × ⅝ in) tongued-and-grooved boarding

**Fascia** 4 off 286 × 57 × 9 mm (11¼ × 2¼ ×
⅜ in) timber

**Roof battens** 2 off 698 × 22 × 22 mm (27½ ×
⅞ × ⅞ in) timber

joints. Drill holes through the legs and, using waterproof glue and zinc-plated screws, glue and screw the bottom of the legs to the bottom of the post. Countersink the screw heads. To start with this construction may look something like an inverted helicopter, but persevere: turn the post around, screwing the legs on one by one.

**2** To many amateur woodworkers one of the greatest drawbacks to building a bird table is the idea that a square hole has to be cut in the centre of the table to accommodate the post. There is no need for any such thing. At the top of the post glue and screw two horizontal battens (bearers). When the table itself is completed, it will be screwed down as a unit to these two horizontal battens.

### THE TABLE

**3** Now for the table. I prefer not to use plywood for outdoor purposes, even plywoods that are sold as exterior grade. Instead I recommend something like Nordic whitewood for the table: it is available in boards of width large enough not to have to go through the irksomely laborious process of jointing two or more together. Thin battens should be glued and screwed all around the top, but with gaps left at the corners to allow the washing down of the table surface in order to clean off unused food and other debris.

*If this is your first woodworking project, you may wish to call it a day at this point.* If you do, just as a final touch add screw eyes to the sides to create the means of attaching bags of nuts and similar goodies. Then screw the table to the horizontal battens on the post. And happy birdwatching.

For those with more confidence – or who are merely more persistent despite everything – having screwed the table to the post, it is time to consider the roof. From the birds' point of view, a roof is a real bonus in wet conditions.

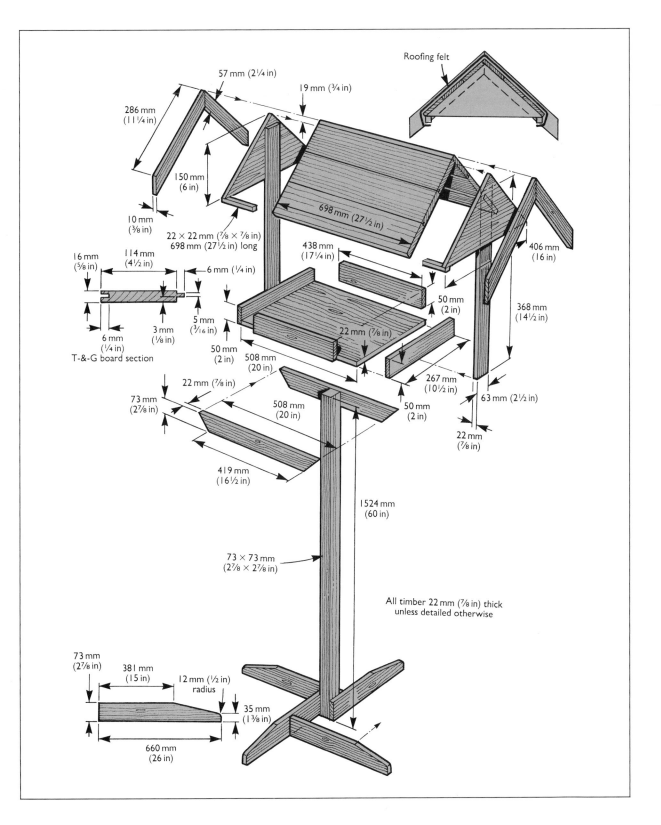

Roofing felt

57 mm (2¼ in)

19 mm (¾ in)

286 mm (11¼ in)

150 mm (6 in)

10 mm (³⁄₈ in)

22 × 22 mm (⁷⁄₈ × ⁷⁄₈ in) 698 mm (27½ in) long

698 mm (27½ in)

438 mm (17¼ in)

406 mm (16 in)

50 mm (2 in)

368 mm (14½ in)

16 mm (⁵⁄₈ in)

114 mm (4½ in)

6 mm (¼ in)

6 mm (¼ in)

3 mm (⅛ in)

5 mm (³⁄₁₆ in)

T-&-G board section

50 mm (2 in)

508 mm (20 in)

22 mm (⁷⁄₈ in)

267 mm (10½ in)

50 mm (2 in)

63 mm (2½ in)

22 mm (⁷⁄₈ in)

22 mm (⁷⁄₈ in)

73 mm (2⁷⁄₈ in)

508 mm (20 in)

419 mm (16½ in)

1524 mm (60 in)

73 × 73 mm (2⁷⁄₈ × 2⁷⁄₈ in)

All timber 22 mm (⁷⁄₈ in) thick unless detailed otherwise

73 mm (2⁷⁄₈ in)

381 mm (15 in)

12 mm (½ in) radius

35 mm (1³⁄₈ in)

660 mm (26 in)

## THE ROOF

**4** The plan is to make the roof before attaching it to the table. Mark out the two triangular pieces of wood to form the ends of the roof. Leave a little of the pencil line showing as you cut, for a smoothing plane will be necessary afterward to remove the saw's roughness. To plane the edges, clamp the triangles and plane both together: that way they will be identical.

The length of the roof between the triangles is made of tongued-and-grooved boards. The tongued-and-grooved boarding may have to be cut down to the correct width: if you find that you have to cut all the way down the length of one board (to get a half-width, say), don't forget to make sure that the tongued-and-grooved edge on the designated piece is the one that fits the adjacent board.

*Above:* The Bird Table requires regular cleaning, and for this purpose clear slots are left around the edge which allow debris to be brushed out and boiling water to be flushed in.
*Right:* It is important that the roof is securely screwed to the table because when winter gales blow a great deal of wind pressure is exerted on the roof.

Place the two triangular roof ends on the workbench; screw the tongued-and-grooved roof lengths to them. Drill a pilot hole for each screw, and countersink at the top – if the screw head is left proud it may in time puncture the covering of roofing felt. To provide a good place to fix the felt, and to add extra rigidity to the roof, glue and screw thin battens of wood to the under edge of the triangular roof sections.
**5** Now fit the roofing felt. For this particular purpose use roofing felt of the lightest weight of the three grades available. The best method is

to fold an edge of the felt and hammer felt-nails through the fold into the batten on the under edge of the roof. Stretch the felt tight up and over the roof ridge and about 7.5 cm (3 in) down the farther slope. Repeat on the other side, and this time once it is stretched over the farther slope nail it down securely there with felt-nails. Then fit the fascia strips.

**6** All that remains is to attach the roof to the table with two vertical slats of wood, one at each side. They too should be screwed in place. But for full weather protection it is best then to seal the side battens and the roofing felt with a bitumastic compound applied with a putty-knife or a plastic spatula. It is essential to prevent water from getting in at the sides.

## FINISHING OFF

The sides and legs of the table, and the post, should similarly be treated with a good wood preservative. Do not, however, treat the surface of the table. In general, wood is quite resistant to rot provided that water is not trapped in cracks or crevices.

Your bird table should be left in place throughout the year. Feeding, however, should take place only during autumn and winter months. At other times – and especially during the breeding season – there should be plenty of natural food sources.

Made in this fashion, a timber bird table should see service for at least 25 years.

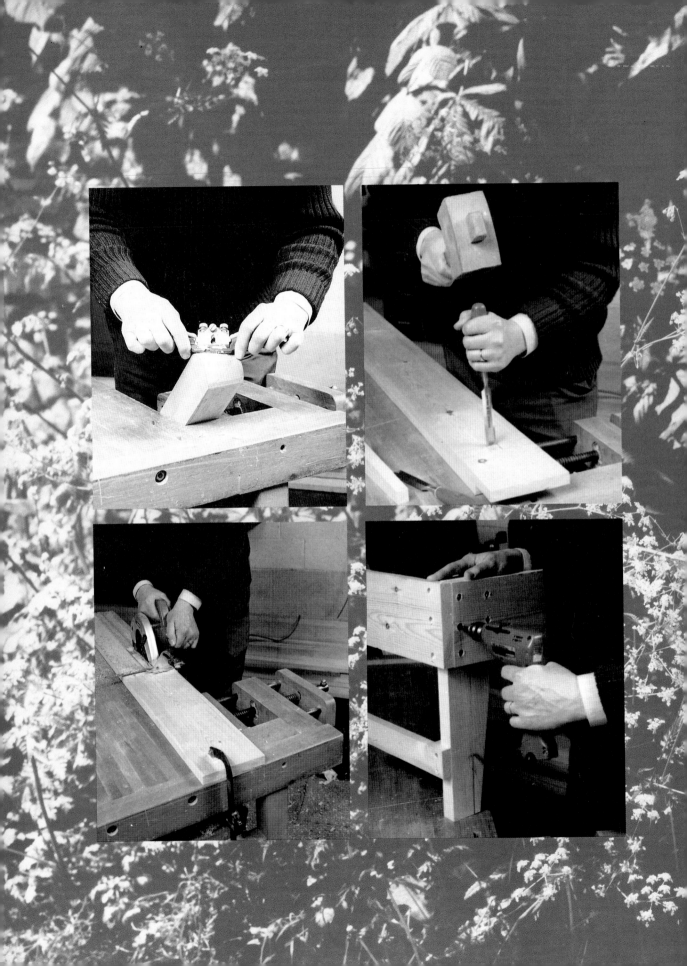

# WHAT TO USE AND HOW TO USE IT

GO INTO ANY DIY STORE AND YOU'LL BE FACED WITH A

CONFUSING MULTITUDE OF MATERIALS AND TOOLS FOR THE

JOB YOU'VE CHOSEN TO DO. TO MAKE THINGS EASIER FOR

YOU, THIS SECTION CONTAINS INFORMATION AND ADVICE

ON MY FAVOURITE TOOLS, AND ON THE VARIOUS MATERIALS

I'VE USED FOR THE PROJECTS IN THE BOOK.

# MATERIALS
# AND TOOLS

In any book that provides technical instructions on a number of projects, the author is faced with the problem of having to repeat instructions over and over again, especially at the end of the projects – as for example in "It is essential that the wood is finally treated with a good wood preservative".

Such phrases tend to be rather vague, whereas most readers would prefer to be able to benefit from the author's advice and personal experience of particular products. I want therefore to be much more specific about the materials and tools I have used on the projects in this book, so that any reader will be able to approach sales staff in a timber yard, DIY store or toolshop and ask knowledgeably for what he or she requires. If the reader still encounters a blank stare of incomprehension, at least he or she can be confident then that it is the sales personnel who do not know enough.

The information I want to pass on also includes safety factors relating to tools, and ecological factors to do with the materials. Readers unused to woodwork may be anxious about injuring themselves with unfamiliar equipment, but may in any case cause themselves harm without being aware of how they might do so.

I am even going to recommend some products by name.

## Wood: the Raw Material

In an age when we are at last waking up to the need to look after our planet, some guidance on timber is of interest to everybody.

For every project in this book I have outlined the sort of wood suitable. In many cases the only real stipulation is that the wood should be free of knots. Plywood and tongued-and-grooved floorboarding feature in a number of projects, sometimes even in combination. Various other boards (such as ship lapboard or match boarding) are suggested and described under only a single project.

But the basic sort of wood that I prefer to have as my standard choice for construction is Nordic whitewood or Nordic redwood. These woods from Sweden and Finland are generally available, in various sizes, are of good quality, and arrive mostly quite dry (unlike some other forms of timber that get to the shops so full of water that they might have been towed behind the ship).

The Nordic redwood (pine wood) saws and planes more easily than the whitewood. Darker in hue, after a period of time in its natural unstained state it turns a rich golden colour. The whitewood is cut from what we know as Christmas trees (those that are allowed to reach full size). It is slightly more tricky to plane smooth, and occasionally contains pockets of resin, but its great advantage is the width of planks in which it is available.

However, the best news is that both Sweden and Finland look after their trees with great care and have for more than a century maintained a careful programme of reafforestation: every year more trees are planted than are cut, thus ensuring that the source is fully sustainable.

## Power Tools

### SCREWDRIVER

The projects in this book rely for their construction not on traditional jointing but on glue and screws. Driving screws into wood by hand – especially when a project requires a large number of screws to be inserted – can be a tedious and even painful task. The invention of the battery-operated (cordless) screwdriver/drill has completely revolutionized my workshop practices. There are no trailing cables that might be inadvertently tripped over or accidentally severed, and even the smallest of the screwdriver/drills now available is capable of more torque (turning power) than most human wrists. Some of these machines drive even the largest screws straight into softwood without any need for a pilot hole to be drilled first. They can reduce the construction time of any one of the projects included in this book by literally hours. The cordless screwdriver/drill that I use is made by Makita.

## SAWS

However, it has to be said that mains-operated electric tools are the standard means of woodworking today. And when it comes to sawing curves (or any awkward shape), the electric jigsaw is unbeatable.

The best types of jigsaw incorporate a plastic safety guard at the front to protect the fingers and hand. Some are able to perform an operation known as sabre-sawing. Sabre-sawing is one of the most valuable functions of a jigsaw, for it allows the operator to start sawing in the middle of a plank, and so to cut slots or holes. This is obviously very useful when you have, for example, to cut a hole for a sink top or cut out a square hole in a door for something like a cat flap. To make a sabre-saw cut, place the saw firmly on its rounded sole plate end, turn the machine on and allow it to run up to full speed. Begin the cut by firmly and slowly pressing the blade down onto the timber at the desired spot, resting the machine all the while on its sole plate. It is this curved end of the sole plate that allows the gentle "rocking" of the blade into the wood. If you don't force the machine, steady pressure is all that is necessary, and the blade will continue to cut steadily right through the plank. It is a good idea to practise this cut on a piece of waste wood, because once you have mastered the technique, it opens all kinds of woodworking possibilities. The electric jigsaw I use has this facility, and is also made by Makita.

Just a bit slower – and therefore just a bit safer – than the circular saw, the jigsaw is probably an ideal first power saw. But for some operations the circular saw is quite the most apt tool. Again, the one I use is made by Makita and has an outstanding safety feature – you cannot start the machine cutting unless both hands are in position on top of the tool. This means that the operator has to fix securely the timber – plywood – he intends to cut before attempting any sawing operation. Safety is also improved by a steel wedge (a "riving knife") which prevents the timber that the blade has cut from then "binding" or clamping on to the blade. If a blade on a machine gets trapped, then a circular saw can buck, and give you a nasty jolt as it attempts to

"climb" out of the wood. As for the blade, one made of tungsten carbide is preferable: it stays sharp for longer than other types, and will cut man-made boards with ease.

## DRILL, PLANE, SANDER

There are many electric drills available. The best have multiple speed control, slow start and can drill forwards or in reverse at the press of a switch. If you anticipate doing a lot of drilling, try to find a quiet one. I can recommend my slimline Makita model.

Far less common is an electric plane. The only problem with this machine is that it is so easy and fast to use that you may find yourself almost at once smoothing sawn timber below your guideline!

Removing saw cuts before you stain, varnish or paint wood is a must. Saw cuts left on edges of board look so very untidy. An electric belt sander will remove large quantities of "wood stock" very quickly. However, for the smaller sanding jobs – finishing timber before painting and rubbing down surfaces between coats of varnish etc. – the little palm sander is ideal. The palm sander is a light tool and, as its name suggests, fits snugly into the hand.

## FIXING AND FIXATIVES

### SCREWS

Almost all of the projects in this book are put together with glue and screws. Screws certainly make for a stronger joint than can be achieved with nails – although nails are indispensable in some building techniques – primarily because the thread of a screw (the ultimate difference between a screw and a nail) helps to clamp firmly together the two pieces of wood being joined. Joining two pieces of wood with nails is not always satisfactory as the joint can become loose.

There are six different things to consider when buying screws in preparation for constructing a project.

**Diameter** This is the figure shown first in the description on a box of screws. So a box marked "8 × 2¼" or "6 × 60" contains screws of 8 G.S. or 6 mm diameter.

**Length** This is the second figure in the description. So a box marked "8 × 2¼" or "6 × 60" contains screws of a length of 2¼ inches or 60 mm.

**Composition** Most screws are made of steel. In this book, however, the screws used are galvanized or brass for weatherproofing or for appearance. It is important to match the composition of the screw with the needs of the project. The type of material that the screw is made from will be shown on the box.

**The screw head**  The countersink screw was the main type of screw head used in this book, although for attaching hinges the round-headed screw was sometimes suggested. There are various other types. Every box of screws has a description of the type within.

**The drive system**  The old-fashioned screw had just a single slot across the top, which allowed the screwdriver to slip if turning became tough. Modern screws are recessed and are cross-headed.

**The finish**  A description on the box will tell you whether the screw has been coated: zinc plating, for example, gives added resistance to corrosion. Zinc-plated screws are recommended for all the projects in this book.

The Supascrew is an ideal general-purpose type of screw: I used it throughout this book.

## COACH-SCREWS AND COACH-BOLTS

Two other fixing devices were used on the projects – coach-screws and coach-bolts.

The coach-screw has a square head, a largely cylindrical shaft, and a short, coarse, screw-thread portion at the base. Once a pilot hole has been drilled, the coach-screw is "started" in the hole, and with a spanner is then "rotated" into the wood. A washer beneath the head gives the screw its maximum clamping potential. The best type of coach-screw is zinc-plated – but these are difficult to obtain. They are available almost exclusively in an ordinary steel finish.

The coach-bolt has a raised, rounded head, beneath which – above the shaft – the shank is square. The square shank locks firmly in the pre-drilled bolt hole and, as the washer and nut are tightened with a spanner at the bottom, prevents the head from turning round. Again, it is difficult to find the best zinc-plated type – the traditional bolt is oily and black, and makes a mess of the wood as you fit it!

## GLUES

There are many types of waterproof glues available. You should try to match the type of glue that is most appropriate to each project you undertake.

First note the difference between "water-resistant" and "waterproof". For the purposes of most of the projects in

this book, water-resistant glue is as good as waterproof ("waterproof" is a term used by manufacturers more for wood joints that are to be immersed in water, as on a boat).

Some glues are bought as powder to be mixed to a paste with water. This type is useful for filling gaps (and so covering up mistakes) and is generally very strong – but a problem can be that you mix up too much or too little at a time. It is available in a variety of quantities.

Ready-mixed glues sold in bottles can be much easier to use, and more economical. Some also come with a non-clog applicator. It is important before buying the glue to read the manufacturer's directions to make sure you are using the glue for a suitable purpose.

In fact it is important to follow the manufacturer's instructions for using all the types of glue.

The glues I used very successfully to make the projects in this book were the two main water-resistant glues produced by Humbrol – Cascamite One-Shot in powder form, and Cascorez ready-mixed.

**That Sinking Feeling: Putting posts in**
Throughout the book I have been singing the praises of the steel sockets with the spiked tip into which posts can be set in the ground. This is because of all the jobs in the garden I really detest, hole digging is at the top of the list. Maybe my dislike really stems from the fact that I am always afraid of getting the hole dug – at tremendous effort – in the wrong place: they should make movable holes specially for garden use!

Fortunately, these sockets are now available (under different names in different countries) and in Britain the major manufacturer is Metpost of Cardiff. They are available in a variety of sizes, e.g. for the Trellis posts right through to the heavyweight sockets needed for the children's Play Tower and for the Barbecue Shelter. The Metpost has welded to its base a 4-square fluted steel spike. To get this beast into the ground all you need is a sledgehammer, with a "driving tool" placed on top of the socket, which prevents the socket from damage as it is forced into the ground. (This driving tool is a piece of oblong indestructible "plastic" which has a steel rod at one end.) The spike is sharp enough to penetrate any kind of soil fairly readily – so be sure to check first that the area chosen is free of electric cables, drainage systems, gas pipes and other potentially expensive errors of judgement. You should also wear heavy-duty gloves.

## WOOD PRESERVATION, STAINS AND VARNISHES

Wood that is thoroughly coated with a good preservative should last a good many years, and if maintained regularly, may last as well as any other fabric exposed to the ravages of wind, rain and frost. Today there is a great variety of wood preservatives available, and for the projects in this book I used quite a number of different brands, each for its specific effect on the particular project.

On projects that may come into contact with pets and plants it is important to use a water-based preservative. For the Bird Table, Nestboxes, Compost Bin and fences I used "Timber Care" by Cuprinol.

Other projects may instead be brushed with a general-purpose clear wood preservative, leaving them in their natural colours to be painted or stained afterwards.

Stains sometimes dry to a surface that is rather oily and may leave marks on hands or clothes that touch them. Wood stain for use on garden furniture should therefore be of the exterior acrylic variety – one of the most advanced wood preservatives – which will not leave a residue on skin or clothes. It dries to a hard semi-transparent finish, allowing the natural character of the wood grain to show through.

One of the manufacturers that produce such advanced stains is Cuprinol: they have also published a useful *Complete Guide to Woodcare* which gives helpful details of the types of wood preservatives on the market.

There are also many different types of all-weather varnish and wood dye, some of which are more suitable for certain projects than others. The range of colours and translucencies is enormous, giving a very wide choice of effects. I particularly like the Furniglass range and used their varnishes on the Letterbox and the Adirondack-style garden chair. In spite of the varnishes being microporous, and thus giving a good sheen, the action of the sunlight will eventually turn the wood beneath to a light greyish colour. To prevent this happening a few drops of a coloured varnish should be added to the clear varnish. This prevents the sun's rays actually reaching the timber and discolouring it.

# INDEX